THE GOLDEN STATE KILLER CASE

50 STATES of CRIME CALIFORNIA

THE GOLDEN STATE KILLER CASE

WILLIAM THORP
TRANSLATED BY LYNN E. PALERMO

CRIME INK
NEW YORK

THE GOLDEN STATE KILLER CASE

Crime Ink
An Imprint of Penzler Publishers
58 Warren Street
New York, N.Y. 10007

© Editions 10/18, Département d'Univers Poche, 2023
In association with So Press/Society
English translation copyright: © 2025 by Lynn E. Palermo

First Crime Ink edition

Cover design by Charles Perry, inspired by the French language
edition cover design by Nicolas Caminade

Interior design by Maria Fernandez

Library of Congress Control Number: 2024919206

ISBN: 978-1-61316-631-4
eBook ISBN: 978-1-61316-632-1

10 9 8 7 6 5 4 3 2 1

Printed in the United States of America
Distributed by W. W. Norton & Company

Contents

PROLOGUE
Rancho Cordova, Spring 1974

A bird's-eye view of Rancho Cordova, California, shows a flat expanse of land with swirls of dotted lines: modest houses packed together like bricks in a wall, and arranged in a network of curved roads and cul-de-sacs. In this part of Sacramento County, all the tract homes are one story and almost identical. They were built so close together that an athletic man could easily leap from one roof to the next for hundreds of yards. The only clue to his passage would be his thudding feet, audible to residents inside the prefab walls. But thanks to the thick shrubbery and oak trees stretching toward the night sky, he'd be as invisible as a cat on the hunt.

One spring evening in 1974, Richard Shelby, aged thirty-six, was in his patrol car, slowly making his rounds. This Rancho Cordova police officer always followed one golden rule. Never turn on lights inside the car. When asked why, he'd reply, "Haven't you heard of the 'Zebra' murders?" It was the police code name used to refer to a gang of African Americans whose members had committed at least fifteen racially motivated murders in the San Francisco Bay area in 1973–74.

Law enforcement had dedicated the entire *Z* frequency to them on the police radio. *Z*, as in *zebra*. Richard Shelby was convinced that killing a white man, in particular a cop, had been the initiation rite into their gang. Never mind that the killings had taken place more than fifty miles to the west or that they had never specifically targeted policemen.

Shelby drove in darkness. For him, it was just more proof that there was always someone out there who wanted to hurt you and that evil was waiting around every corner. On this evening, most of the houses were enveloped in a darkness that the moon dared not penetrate, and the rare pedestrians out late only appeared in his field of vision at the last moment, dazed by his headlights.

Police radio static shattered the routine calm. A couple on Dolcetto Street had just called the sheriff's department. The husband was concerned about noises coming from the house next door, which was supposed to be empty. The department had sent out two units. Shelby was only a few houses away, so, in a tone that discouraged all refusal, he informed the dispatcher that he was on his way over there too.

When he arrived, one of his fellow officers was already there, talking to the couple. Suspicious noises had come from the backyard of the house next door, but these neighbors hadn't seen anyone come or go. The officers decided to split up to walk the premises. Shelby and another officer went through the backyard while the third officer inspected the front of the house. None of them observed any trace of infraction. Even so, they walked the perimeter a second time. They found no evidence of a burglar or prowler, so they left.

Shelby had only driven a couple blocks when his radio crackled again. The couple on Dolcetto Street had just seen a figure fleeing from the house next door. Shelby made a U-turn.

Just after the officers left, the husband explained he heard the noise again. Then, up on his neighbor's roof, he saw a man dressed in military fatigues. The individual was around five feet, ten inches tall with blond hair. He looked fairly young, around twenty. He must have been up there the whole time the police were inspecting the area, watching them work and protected by the darkness. As soon as he saw them leave, he jumped off the roof. "With the ease of a cat," added the worried neighbor.

Shelby went back to the neighbor's house. The garage door was open. Earlier, it had been shut. Going in, Shelby stumbled over a piece of firewood about two feet long and almost entirely covered with a dark, sticky substance. Blood. So much of it that he could hardly see the wood. Shelby glanced around the garage, then decided to go in, without notifying headquarters. He didn't want to get bogged down with more officers and dozens of rotating lights. Shelby had always been a loner. When he had to go in, he did it on his own, with a hand on his nine-millimeter service pistol.

He climbed the several steps leading from the garage into the house. As he made his way from room to room with his flashlight turned off, the house looked neat and well-kept. Nothing seemed out of place. No bodies to indicate where the blood on the log had originated.

Shelby opened the door to the last room, the master bedroom. Everything seemed in order. He took a step toward the nightstand. That's when he saw a small, dark mass on the floor at the foot of the bed. Shelby shone his flashlight on it. A puppy. The small animal had been beaten so violently and with so many blows—probably with that hunk of wood—that its intestines were spilling across the floor. Half-hidden under the bed, it looked like the frightened thing had tried to hide underneath. The officer scanned the room one more time. Only one silhouette could be seen in the light filtering in from outside, and that was his own. The man on the roof had vanished.

The detective quickly connected this massacred puppy to other cases. For two years, a burglar had been leap-frogging from house to house in Rancho Cordova, leaving dead dogs in his wake. Police officers had heard reports of dogs being attacked and dogs left to bleed to death in stairways and living rooms. One time, the local newspaper, *The Grapevine*, had even published a photo of a wiry chocolate Labrador named Pups that had been killed in its yard. That was February 1972. The prowler had broken its ribs, jaw, and teeth with a thick piece of firewood.

The perpetrator acted at night and wasn't satisfied with just killing dogs. He also broke into houses but was so discreet that the next day, victims felt like they'd been robbed by a ghost. With him circulating in the area, people began to fear the silence. Town residents and the media started calling him the "Cordova Cat Burglar." The statistics were remarkable. In just the first six months of 1973, he had entered more than fifty homes—sometimes several in a single night. The type of items stolen was intriguing. Usually, the burglar ignored items of value and stole only trinkets, as if the burglary were just an excuse to intrude. Occasionally, couples woke up late at night to find an intruder staring at them silently. One night, a woman surprised him as he was leaning over her, stroking her breast.

For a long time, Shelby thought these burglaries were the work of troubled adolescents. But that evening, beneath the halo of the streetlights, the police officer had his doubts. A teenager wouldn't massacre a dog like that. If he did, it would mean he was dangerous.

Shelby didn't realize at that moment that decades later, he would think back on this incident, wishing he could go back in time and do things differently. He wouldn't have played the lone cowboy. He would have called in all reinforcements. He would have ripped every single shingle off the roof. He would have shaken down every bush, every tree. He would have lit up the whole crime scene like high noon that spring night. He would have done anything to avoid giving that intruder who had watched him from the rooftop a chance to flee. For on this day in 1974, that very same man was preparing to plunge Sacramento County into a decade of terror.

I DARK OF NIGHT
1976–1979

Chapter 1

With its long windows, narrow like arrow slits, the Sacramento County Sheriff's Office looked like an impregnable castle. It was located at 711 G Street, in the heart of California's capital city. The message it communicated couldn't be clearer: County law enforcement starts here, and the law will not be disputed. Offices on the third floor dealt with murder, burglary, and minor misdemeanors.

This was where Richard Shelby now worked, in an office barely large enough to squeeze in a small table and chair. If you leaned in from the corridor, you'd see his six-foot, three-inch frame hunched over a gray Royal typewriter sitting on the table. Usually, he wore a short-sleeved white shirt with a psychedelic necktie. He had black hair combed over to the right side in a wave, with sideburns stretching down his jawline, as fashion dictated.

Since the days of patrolling the neighborhoods in Rancho Cordova two years before, the former patrol officer had earned a promotion and was now inspector. He was a man with a reputation for being a formidable investigator. The type who dove into neighborhood trash barrels, if necessary, and turned over the city from one end to the other for clues. Nowhere did Richard Shelby feel more at home than in the streets of Sacramento County, pounding the asphalt and banging on doors with his fist. He had the fiery temperament of a person who explodes if he's shut up in an office.

On an October morning in 1976, sitting in the sheriff's department cafeteria, Shelby was blowing on his cup of coffee to cool it down. He was half listening to the chatter between those coming in to start their day and those who were headed home to get some sleep after being on duty all night. That day, one voice rose above all the others. Captain Stamm, a Korean War veteran with thinning hair, was telling everyone that a young woman had just been attacked at her home in the Sacramento suburb of Citrus Heights. She'd been tied up, gagged, and raped. No trace of the attacker. A police officer was already on the scene, but two other detectives were needed to join him. The captain pointed at Shelby, now thirty-eight, and thirty-six-year-old Carol Daly, a detective with deep blue eyes.

The two investigators jumped in the car and drove the fifteen miles separating the northern part of the city from this middle-class suburb similar to Rancho Cordova. It had neighborhoods of one-story houses with modestly sloped roofs and front doors that opened to the street like so many invitations. The sun was already high in the sky by the time they pulled up in front of a low, narrow white house on Wood-park Way. The garage swallowed half the front; in the backyard, an inflatable swimming pool indicated the presence of small children. Jane, the victim, was at her neighbor's house. Her hair was disheveled, and her shirt was discolored with red stains. Her wrists were still bleeding from being so tightly bound. With her gaze fixed on the ground, she began relating the events of that morning.

Her husband, a captain in the Air Force, had left for work at about 6:30 A.M. Her three-year-old son had climbed into bed with her to snuggle. Only a few minutes later, she heard the door to the garage shut and someone running up the hallway. She thought maybe her husband had forgotten something. Then her bedroom door flew open, and a man wearing a ski mask burst into the room, wielding a butcher knife.

Jane screamed. He fell on top of her, hissing through clenched teeth, "Shut up! I just want your money. I'm not going to hurt you. Shut up and don't move. I'll stab you if you don't cooperate." He added, "If you don't do what I tell you, I'll kill you and your son."

The man in the ski mask pulled out black shoelaces and bound Jane's wrists together using a diamond knot—a sailor's knot. He gagged the woman and the child, blindfolded them both, and tied their ankles together. Jane remembered rolling slowly over on the bed, wanting to touch her son and comfort him—but not feeling him there. *What's he done with him? Is he still alive? Is he going to kill us both?* she wondered as the burglar rummaged around in the closets, muttering unintelligibly. She listened to his muffled steps leave and then come back into the bedroom. Then she felt a dab of something greasy in her bound hands, like hand lotion.

The man said, "Play with it."

Jane obeyed. Then he untied her feet. She clearly remembered thinking, *Oh my God, I am going to be raped.*

Shelby and Daly took down the victim's statement. After the rape, Jane told them, the attacker went into the kitchen. She could hear him rummaging in the refrigerator and shoving pots and pans around. He seemed to be cooking something. Finally, after a half hour of silence, she was able to work herself out of her gag and pull the blindfold down off her eyes. Jane saw her son lying a few yards away, asleep. She woke him up, and with their ankles still bound, mother and son hopped to the sliding glass door at the back of the house. It only took a few minutes for the neighbor to come to their rescue.

While Daly was taking the rest of her statement, Shelby went over to inspect the area around the house. He walked back up to Shadowbrook Way, the street that ran along the other side of Jane's house, after an empty lot. A resident on that street told him a green Chevrolet coupe had been parked there that morning. The sergeant also learned that a strange burglar had struck in the area during the preceding weeks. He'd stolen trinkets and costume jewelry from one house, then deposited them in another, where he had again stolen items with no monetary value. It was as if he was trading the belongings of one house for those of another.

Jane had been one of those victims. The offender had stolen a pair of her earrings and a bracelet. She wouldn't even have noticed if she hadn't found costume jewelry that didn't belong to her lying beside her jewelry box. The burglar had entered through her son's room, just like the rapist.

When Shelby returned to Jane's house, he looked concerned. He wondered if this was more than just another crime in a city with its share of fractured destinies and interrupted lives. The man in the dark ski mask had none of the characteristics of a criminal who acted on impulse. He knew the husband's routine, knew where to enter the house, and knew how to escape without being seen. That wasn't how a classic rapist operated. Shelby had a sense of foreboding. Whether there in the quiet streets of Citrus Heights or elsewhere in the United States, this man had committed rape before.

Back on the third floor at the sheriff's department, Sergeant Shelby asked around the office if anyone had worked on any rape cases recently with a victim like Jane—a young woman bound, gagged, and raped—and with a suspect who hid behind a ski mask.

A colleague told him about a case on Paseo Drive in Rancho Cordova. On June 18, a young woman, twenty-two, had awakened to a man standing in her bedroom, staring at her. He was wearing a dark blue T-shirt and a white hand-knit ski mask. He bound her wrists together so tightly that she felt like her hands had been amputated. He had a small penis, which he had lubricated himself, with Johnson's Baby Oil. There was also a fifteen-year-old girl who'd felt a man lie down on top of her in the middle of the night. That was on July 17 at about two o'clock in the morning. The teenager lived in Carmichael, a town about a fif-teen-minute drive from the first victim. Her parents were away on a four-day hike. The man tied the teen's hands together, then pressed against her from behind. He said, "Play with it."

Another detective told Shelby about a mother, aged forty, on Malaga Way in Rancho Cordova. She had been awakened by her twelve-year-old daughter, who had seen a man in a ski mask staring at her through her open bedroom window. The mother went to the girl's room to check and saw no one but smelled aftershave lotion. Immediately, she ran to her second daughter's bedroom to get her out of bed. When she went back into the first room, the man was staring at her through the window. A moment later, he was behind her in the hallway, holding a pistol. He was wearing a ski mask but no pants or underpants. The woman fought him off, and he fled.

Finally, a twenty-nine-year-old woman, also in Car-michael, had been attacked in her home by a man wearing a gray ski mask and armed with a knife. That incident had taken place a month earlier, on September 4. The rapist had bound her wrists with white laces and told her, "Do it right or I'll kill you."

The same MO, the same man, about five feet, ten inches tall, ski mask, same threats, same obsession with hand lotion, same suburbs on the east side of Sacramento. Shelby took the stories like so many punches to the gut. He no longer heard the strident ring of the telephones, the discussions playing out around him, or the clacking of typewriters. He turned to his colleagues and said, "I think we have a fucking serial rapist on our hands."

On the third floor, the detectives were all crowded into cramped offices, while the fourth floor housed the sheriff's department big shots. Shelby knew he wasn't welcome up there. His relations with the hierarchy—especially the deputy sheriff—were fractious, poisoned by years of high words and low blows. Shelby had the reputation of being a hothead, so when he informed the lieutenant of what he had learned, he wasn't surprised to see the lieutenant remain impassive and nod, without asking questions. He said he would talk it over with the ranking officers on the fourth floor. Later, Shelby received Sheriff Duane Lowe's reply. "We're not communicating the facts to anyone. This man has to be arrested before the affair gets out and frightens the city."

The journalists, whose relationship with the police was intertwined like wisteria on the wall of an old house, were also briefed. They were forbidden to publish any information on the rapist and instructed to let any rumors die on their own in order to protect the investigation and avoid inciting copycat crimes. The cops said they would apprehend the offender soon, and the story could be published at that time.

But soon, two events happened that turned everything upside down.

The first took place on October 9, four days after Jane was raped. A nineteen-year-old woman was attacked in Rancho Cordova at 4:30 A.M. by a man wearing a ski mask. Then, on October 18, two other women were raped, one in Carmichael and the other in Rancho Cordova. They lived only a few minutes apart, as the crow flies.

Shelby felt himself losing his grip on the case. The situation was beginning to explode, and rumors were beginning to fly. Had citizens been warned about what was happening in their streets at night, these three attacks could have been avoided. Sheriff Lowe had no other choice but to go public with the case. He asked

Shelby and Daly to organize two community meetings. The first took place on November 3 at the Del Dayo Elementary School in Carmichael. Five hundred people showed up. They looked dressed up for an evening out. Many of the men had come straight from the office and were still wearing their white shirts, jackets, and ties. The women's hairdos looked perfect. Some of the couples had brought notebooks to take down information.

Carol Daly opened the meeting. She passed over the details but confirmed the facts. A man was attacking women in Sacramento County at night. "This man is a rapist. He is dangerous. He enters the house through the windows that you leave open, through the doors that you leave unlocked. He finds the extra key that you leave in your mailbox or hide under a rock for your children. He knows how you live, he knows your habits. Close the curtains. Lock yourselves in. Keep an eye on your neighborhood and call us if you suspect anything."

A few hours later, the local newspaper, *The Sacramento Bee*, went to press. At the top of the legal column, the headline read "Man Hunted as Suspect in 8 Rapes." The journalists had also dubbed the offender "The East Area Rapist."

Chapter 2

Richard Shelby lived in Rancho Cordova, right in the heart of the perpetrator's zone of predilection. He lived at 2308 El Manto Drive with his wife Eleanor and their two sons, Brian and Tom, in a one-story house with several bedrooms and a living room with stacks of books. In the backyard was a stone barbecue built by the detective and a stretch of greenery as big as a football field. It was a suburban family home typical of a calm, prosperous America.

Except that Shelby had cursed this neighborhood since the day he'd moved in, even before the East Area Rapist prowled there at night. Now he liked it even less. He couldn't stand the houses being lined up like a perfect set of teeth. Or the residents' habit of checking out their neighbors' interiors as they strolled past their picture window in the evening. Shelby preferred open air, empty spaces, living where you heard people approaching from their tires crunching in the gravel. He had spotted such a house farther east, in the Nevada desert, but his wife had refused to move there. She worried about nocturnal visitors.

Shelby had grown up in Central California in the San Joaquin Valley, a corner of the desert like the one he had his eye on. It was a vast stretch filled with wheat fields and only a handful of towns, including McSwain, where he'd lived. It wasn't much more than a grocery store surrounded by a few farms. The Shelbys lived in an old dairy, whose thick wooden doors, along with the three mammoth eucalyptus trees out back, served as a local landmark.

Like Richard's father, a hard man born in Oklahoma, the residents of McSwain were immersed in the myth of the Wild West and did their best to live it faithfully. Out there, men didn't cry. They shot first and asked questions later. The work turned their hands to leather. They kept their feelings in a safe with the key thrown away. Children were reared on the same myth. By the age of ten, Shelby and his pals were walking to school with a pistol tucked in their belts. The teacher just asked them to place their guns next to the wall in the classroom and leave them alone during the day. A man was not to be deprived of his gun, not even at ten years of age. Walking home after school, the boys shot up bushes or hunted small animals.

Among these tough men with their tales and exploits, Richard soon found a role model, his uncle Hoyt. He was a man who had started with nothing the century before and grown up to become sheriff by dint of his courage and perseverance. Uncle Hoyt knew no fear. Shelby still remembered riding in his uncle's car the day of that big storm. The wind battered the vehicle, rain pounded the windshield, and flashes of lightning obliterated their view of the road. But the old man just kept driving along, like nothing was wrong. When lightning struck a telephone pole right next to them, Uncle Hoyt even laughed as he twisted the steering wheel to prevent the car from swerving and continued on his way, unfazed. That day, Richard Shelby decided that when he grew up, he would be like his uncle Hoyt.

So, after graduating high school, no one was surprised when he set out to pass the police academy entrance exam. He had two wishes: to wear the uniform and to be assigned to a county as far away from center-city Sacramento as possible. Both proved elusive. He'd lost the

end of the middle finger on his left hand when a friend
accidentally shot him during one of their hunting expeditions. And the rules were clear: Police officers had to
have all ten fingers to wear the badge. However, the day
after that setback, they called him back in. The United
States was engaged in a war in Vietnam. Every day, GIs
came home either rattled or in a coffin. Police departments were experiencing a shortage of officers. Richard
would do, after all. On August 1, 1966, he was officially
named officer of the law. But he didn't get everything:
He was assigned to center-city Sacramento.

For the past ten years, Shelby had been crisscrossing
the region, learning every corner of the area between
his place of work and his home. And yet, the East Area
Rapist continued to elude him. Shelby had even tacked
a map of the county to his office wall. Each red pin
represented one of the eight victims. He noticed the
rapist's hunting grounds formed a small arc that could
be traveled by car in scarcely fifteen minutes. The perpetrator never strayed far from the towns of Rancho
Cordova, Carmichael, and Citrus Heights, all three of
them suburbs of Sacramento.

And he moved about as if he'd known the area since
childhood. From the way he arrived undetected and
then vanished, Shelby deduced that the attacker knew

all the avenues, passages, canals, and even underground rain sewer pipes like the back of his hand. Shelby was convinced the man was from the area. In fact, he might still live there.

Since the East Area Rapist had struck for the ninth time in Citrus Heights the previous November 10, this time his victim a sixteen-year-old girl. Sheriff Lowe no longer wanted to waste time. He set up a task force dedicated to tracking down the rapist. The team consisted of over forty people: investigators, a tactical intervention team, a canine squad, a forensics team, and a street team that dressed in plain clothes to blend in with the public or to hide down in ditches or up in trees, waiting desperately in the dark for the offender to show. They were nicknamed the "X-ray Units."

Two detectives, a man and a woman, even occupied a house in Rancho Cordova for a while. They mimicked normal life during the day and slept there at night, hoping to attract the attention of the East Area Rapist. Carol Daly was on the task force. Her presence at crime scenes and the town halls, which she organized, made her one of the public faces of the investigation. As for Shelby, he rode alone. His superiors granted him free rein to investigate on his own. He was instructed to continue making his rounds, question people in the street, and analyze every location where the criminal had intruded. He was given carte blanche.

Shelby visited the crime scenes again and again. He understood that the prowler usually slipped into the residences through the backyard. He climbed over the fence, then hid in the bushes, waiting for the right moment. The perpetrator seemed familiar with his victims' schedule, which meant he either knew them personally or had cased them for days. The East Area Rapist did not attack at random. He often telephoned his victims in the days preceding his strike. They would hear a few seconds of heavy breathing on the line, then the phone hung up on the other end.

He also broke into homes as a prelude to his attacks. He ransacked them, moving objects about, digging through underwear drawers, and stealing jewelry. Sometimes the stolen objects were later recovered under the eaves of a house nearby. Shelby couldn't figure out why until he finally realized that the perpetrator wasn't tossing them from the other yard—they were falling out of his pockets as he crawled across the roof.

Victim testimony allowed the detective to construct a composite police sketch of the rapist in a ski mask. He looked like Everyman, almost: about twenty years of age, around five feet, ten inches tall, medium build.

Distinctive features included hairy legs with muscular calves and a small penis. His deep voice sometimes sounded forced. Occasionally, he stuttered or muttered to himself, as if waging some internal battle. His MO had remained constant since the beginning. He attacked while his victims were sleeping and bound their wrists, his face hidden behind a ski mask. After committing the rapes, he ransacked the houses and cooked himself a meal, emptying kitchen cabinets. Sometimes, he also downed a few beers.

Who could he be? Shelby noted that the man he was after had a penchant for trellises and khaki clothes. He was good with a knife and tied knots that were impossible to loosen. His hypothesis inched along. Was he a military man? A Vietnam veteran? In the area around Sacramento, there were five military bases. Just a few minutes from Rancho Cordova, several thousand soldiers were deployed at Mather Air Force Base alone. That might explain how the perpetrator was able to disappear so quickly into the natural surroundings after committing the crimes.

Shelby wasn't the only one to think of this. The sheriff's department contacted a colonel in the Green Berets and invited him to come advise the detectives. The colonel told them, "Look where you think he won't be. Look up on the roof, in the bushes, in the trees. Look in the most unexpected places, and if you don't see him, that doesn't mean he's not watching you at that very moment. If he is trained, he can hold the same position for hours, without any sound or movement. Think of him like a snake or a leopard, crouching in the shadows, waiting for his moment."

Shelby was juggling all these factors in his mind when he was summoned to another crime scene at 9:00 P.M. on December 18, 1976.

The victim's name was Kris MacFarlane. She was fifteen years old. She had been practicing the piano at home while her parents were out at a Christmas party when she felt a cold blade at her throat. Then heard these words spoken quickly:

"Get up, and if you try anything, I will slide this knife across your throat and disappear into the night."

The man bound her wrists together with shoelaces and dragged her out to the backyard, where he made her sit on a bench. For the next several minutes, she could hear him back inside, in the kitchen, slamming cupboard doors and rummaging through drawers. Then he came back out to her and made her his tenth victim.

Chapter 3

The weeks passed in a string of headlines. On January 24, 1977, *The Sacramento Bee* front page read "Rapist Strikes Again." On February 7, "15th Assault: East Area Rapist Attacks?" On March 8, "Rape May Be Linked to Series?"

By spring 1977, the list of offenses committed by the East Area Rapist was terrifying. Fourteen rapes had been recorded by the police in nine months. After each one, the sheriff's department spokesperson went before the press and observed resignedly, "It's the same MO as in the other crimes." Among themselves, investigators were beginning to take the perpetrator's mantra before each attack seriously. "I'll be gone in the dark."

The city turned into a fortress. Windows that used to stay open all night to welcome cool breezes coming off the American River were now locked tight. Doors were bolted. Hardware stores bustled with customers wanting stronger, more sophisticated locks and the latest alarm systems. Some homeowners even installed wrought iron bars at their windows and bought watchdogs.

Police officers specializing in security offered community sessions to instruct residents on how to secure their homes with whatever means they had at hand. One suggested, "Fasten little bells to doors and windows. Install wires across doorways and attach them to your nightstand so you'll know if someone has entered your home."

At night, helicopters patrolled overhead, their blades chopping the air. Residents could see them projecting searchlights so powerful that their beams pierced the privacy of darkness in the yards and woods around the houses.

Inside houses, residents took the same precautions and used the same tricks. They hid baseball bats, hammers, and handguns under mattresses. In one house, the residents piled their beds high with clothes and overcoats, hoping it would look like nobody was sleeping under the covers. In another home, the family set up a system of guard duty so one of the two adults was always alert. In a third house, the father slept on the living room sofa, gun in hand, ready to detect the slightest attempt at intrusion. Another family moved out of the house completely, renting a room in a motel. They told their neighbors they'd be back when the perpetrator was arrested.

Gun sales skyrocketed. Five thousand more sold in the county than the year before. In neighborhoods where nights had always been quiet, residents sometimes heard gunshots echoing through normally tranquil Sacramento suburbs. Sometimes the targets were husbands coming home drunk or young people coming home after a party. Mailmen, milkmen, and gardeners also paid the price. In the early morning hours, they were met on front porches with suspicion by homeowners hiding a gun behind their backs.

Vigilant citizens, equipped with CB radios, organized patrols. Among themselves, they called their association the "EARS Patrol," East Area Rapist Surveillance Patrol, and inscribed it on their cars in large letters, like a message intended for the rapist. *The Sacramento Bee* carried their ad offering a $15,000 reward for any information leading to the criminal's arrest. In one of the county towns, someone hung a mannequin wearing a ski mask from a tree with a cord knotted around its neck. The pink sign affixed to it read "East Area Rapist."

In March 1977, Richard Shelby was sitting on the hood of his Dodge, one foot on the ground and the other perched on the bumper. He had cut the motor and flipped off the headlights, so he'd be swallowed by the night. He was posted in front of the American River, which was bordered by thick conifers and sycamores with limbs spread wide. The river flowed between the towns of Rancho Cordova and Carmichael, separating the two. This was an ideal spot to slip from one town to the other undetected. Shelby was convinced this was the route the East Area Rapist took after committing his crimes, so this was the spot he'd decided to stake out.

He'd managed to dig up a thermal camera, which gave him the ability to see in the dark as well as he would in full daylight. Through the viewfinder, he searched for red vapors given off by a warm body, which could be detected dozens of yards away. He examined every oak tree, every movement in the water, and everything the moon illuminated on the ground. He listened attentively to the silence. Surely, at some point, a person's breath would break the apparent calm.

While waiting, Shelby mulled things over. Maybe he'd missed something. Why that house? Why that woman? In his mind, he kept going back to the fourteen case reports, opening them, closing them, opening them again. He already knew every page. He slept with them and woke up with them. By morning, he was up-to-date and could recite passages from them to his wife, Eleanor, over breakfast.

Then he climbed behind the wheel of his car and drove up and down Woodpark Way, El Segundo Drive, and Ladera Way—the streets where the rapes had been committed. He drove those streets over and over again. Criminals always returned to the scenes of their crimes. Every face, every figure he encountered, he viewed as a possible suspect. He followed every conceivable lead, including the unlikely ones, even the impossible ones. Like the guy whose neighbors reported having a persistent stare, or somebody's brother "who's not so clearheaded," or the guy who lives on the corner, "and if you want my opinion, you should probably question him." Sometimes the leads gave him hope. More often, they died in the blink of an eye.

There was an Arthur P., who at around five feet, ten inches tall, with black hair and blue eyes, looked like a guy up to no good. When the police stopped by to talk to him, he had a concealed knife in a leather sheath. His record revealed an arrest in the 1960s for several rapes in Sacramento, and he was officially deemed a "mentally disturbed sexual delinquent." Arthur P. had been in Vietnam. Shelby surveilled him for entire days, then weeks. Nothing conclusive.

Then there was the priest who'd been stopped by the California Highway Patrol after he'd been stalking a girl outside an Irish pub in Fair Oaks, north of Rancho Cordova. The man of faith had tailed the young woman all the way to her house before driving away.

Another one was B., a thirty-five-year-old male, about five feet, ten inches tall, with light brown hair, who had been arrested after holding a young woman prisoner for three hours in Sacramento County. He had tied her up and blindfolded her.

And so many others. Dozens, hundreds. Men who fit the description and had imperfect lives. Shelby waited for them to take a wrong step—in vain.

Nine months had gone by and still no apprehension. Sometimes, Shelby wondered if he was a lousy cop or if the East Area Rapist was some kind of evil genius. He could find excuses, like the outdated police service he had inherited, which had eroded over time. When Shelby began his career, the department was under the control of John Misterly, alias "Big John," a man who weighed 285 pounds, had the face of a rabid dog, and managed the four floors of the department with an iron fist. The sheriff had built his reputation by chasing the Hell's Angels out of the county. He was an officer who was effective in his brutality and who didn't worry about the rest.

By the time he left in the early 1970s, the police department's equipment had deteriorated. The armory was stacked high with Thompson rifles dating back to the 1920s. Only one squad car was equipped with a gooseneck lamp capable of lighting up the street like midday. Add to that the competition among the various county services. Some kept the information they collected under lock and key so they could be the ones to break the case. Other officers just forgot to share information or even spoiled leads through incompetence.

Shelby was still brooding over the day a twenty-year-old man called the department to tell them he'd found a bag stashed in his backyard containing a ski mask, gloves, and a flashlight. Exactly like the ski mask rapist. But the officer who handled the call tersely instructed him just to "throw it out."

If only Shelby had fingerprints to work with. The crime scenes had all been examined with magnifying glass and dusted with powder to reveal traces, but the East Area Rapist had left none. Not a single time, not even on the bodies of the women he assaulted. He rarely took off his gloves to touch them. Ideally, they would catch him in the act, but despite scrutinizing all the police reports, analyzing every trace of the offender's passage, penetrating his MO, and memorizing the locations of his strikes, Shelby never managed to stake out the right location.

The rapist evaded the police ambushes as though able to figure them out ahead of time—to the point where Shelby sometimes felt like the man was always nearby and listening over his shoulder. What if the East Area Rapist was a Sacramento County police officer?

There was a story that fed that suspicion. One evening, a woman thought she'd seen someone prowling around her house on Sunrise Boulevard, near the American River. Shelby was the first officer to arrive on the scene, but when the woman opened her door, she was startled to see him. She thought a policeman was already searching the area for the intruder. A few minutes earlier, she'd heard a police radio outside her window.

One of the only leads held by the department was a drop of blood belonging to the rapist, which had been recovered from a victim's hair. Presumably, he'd injured himself while assaulting her. Based on Shelby's suspicions, the decision was made to analyze the blood group of about a hundred county police officers whose physical features more or less corresponded to the police sketch of the East Area Rapist. All submitted to the procedure. A few days later, the results came back. Negative. None of those who shared the same blood type as the attacker was the rapist. If the perpetrator was a policeman, he wasn't on the force in Sacramento.

Pursuing the East Area Rapist, Shelby sometimes felt like he was chasing a mirage. A man with no face, no name, no past. And yet, in the preceding few weeks, his hope had rekindled. The detective now had a new police sketch in his hands. In that one, the suspect, dressed in military fatigues, was squinting and had a thin strand of hair combed to one side. The lead had been brought by two investigators in Visalia, a four-hour drive from Sacramento. The investigators told Shelby it might be the face of the East Area Rapist.

Chapter 4

John Vaughan had the massive build of a stereotypical rural American raised on beef and corn. William (Bill) McGowen, somewhat younger at around thirty, wore his dark hair combed over to one side and slicked down. His voice was low, and his lips barely moved as he spoke. They were two different kinds of cops, but they were bringing Shelby the same message: Downstate, where they worked, they had a case very similar to the one terrorizing Sacramento County. They had named their perpetrator the "Visalia Ransacker."

Three years earlier, in April 1974, to be exact, things had started near the College of the Sequoias. From then on, every week, and soon every evening, a strange burglar had entered empty homes in the housing development.

He never stole anything of value but instead trashed the rooms. He ruined clothes, disturbed people's belongings, and even stranger, seemed obsessed with family photos. He moved them around, cut them up, tore them out of frames and hurled the frames against the walls, and then stole the portraits he found appealing.

The intruder also seemed to have a fascination for women's underwear. He pulled them out of the drawers and laid them out on the beds, as if creating a silhouette, or else lined them up on the floor down the hallway, like a trail to be followed. Sometimes the families found traces of sperm in the bedrooms and noticed that someone had used their hand lotion.

The burglar started out visiting one, maybe two, houses per week, but then the pace accelerated. Sometimes four, five, or six houses. In fifteen months, over eighty homes had been burgled. The record number was thirteen houses ransacked in two days over Thanksgiving weekend. The MO was always the same: The intruder planned his strikes, made sure to have an easy escape route, and often balanced china teacups on doorknobs or tipped chairs against the doors. The sound of china shattering soon became an alarm for area residents because it meant the Visalia Ransacker was in the neighborhood.

Then, continued Vaughan and McGowen, on September 11, 1975, the case took on new dimensions. At two o'clock in the morning, a sixteen-year-old girl felt a hand stuffing a gag in her mouth. A man in a black ski mask was standing there, a revolver in his hand. He ordered the young girl to follow him into the backyard. The noise awakened the girl's father, Claude Snelling, who was a professor of journalism. When he rushed out into the backyard, the intruder shot him twice. Then he pointed the revolver at the young woman, but instead of shooting, he struck her with the gun and fled on foot. Claude Snelling died in the ambulance on the way to the hospital. That evening, the Visalia Ransacker's status changed. He was now a murderer.

Investigators dissected his earlier burglaries again, as well as the larger crime scenes. They examined every trace of his movements, every footprint. Dr. Joel Fort, a leading psychiatrist who would gain fame two years later for his interviews with Charles Manson, was charged with analyzing the murderer's behavior. Dr. Fort constructed a portrait of a "suspect who is primarily a prowler and a Peeping Tom," for whom "burglary is secondary" and whose "primary motivation for the crime is sexual. He doesn't call attention to himself [. . .] but is kind of reclusive, isolated, and has no obvious or known friendships or social relations. It has to be someone who has lived in the area for a long time, but the neighbors know little about him. A loner."

Bill McGowen, the young cop from Visalia, learned from other parents that footprints had been found three times under their nineteen-year-old daughter's window on West Kaweah Avenue.

McGowen set up a stakeout in the next-door neighbor's garage that looked out onto the street. At nightfall, he caught sight of a shadowy figure walking past the front of the garage and creeping along the outside of the house toward the backyard. He was stocky and wearing blue jeans, a flak jacket, and a black ski mask shoved up on his forehead. McGowen was certain he was staring at the Visalia Ransacker. Drawing his service revolver, he approached quietly and aimed his weapon at the prowler.

"Oh my God! Please don't hurt me!" the subject shrieked, moving slowly with each word, one step forward, back, to the side.

"Police officer! I told you to put your hands up! Stop or I'll shoot!" the officer warned him.

"Look! My hands are up!" he squealed as he raised his right hand. As he did this, he dug around in his jacket with his left hand. He pulled his own pistol from his jacket pocket and fired a shot at the cop. Instantly, the two men were plunged into darkness. The prowler's shot had hit McGowen's flashlight.

The sound of the gunshot alerted one of the other cops, who radioed in an alert. "The Visalia Ransacker is in the area. Set up roadblocks." Soon, over forty police officers had locked down the neighborhood, including with police dogs on leashes. They searched behind every bush, but the attacker had vanished.

A little over a year later, the three investigators met in person in Richard Shelby's tiny office. The Sacramento sergeant listened attentively to the two officers who had come from Visalia. A burglar who stole nothing, a perverse fascination for feminine undergarments, the use and abuse of his victims' lotions, and the dark ski mask with holes for his eyes. All this corresponded to the man he was tracking and not finding. He studied the police sketch that the Visalia cops had brought along. The almond eyes, full cheeks, and straw-colored hair brushed to one side did not impress him. He felt like he was looking at an adolescent who might be picked up for loitering in a doughnut shop.

He asked the two investigators what had happened after their face-to-face incident with the perpetrator. The detectives sighed. In heavy voices, they told him that after that incident, they suspected the Visalia

Ransacker of burglarizing two other houses before he disappeared.

His police sketch had now been published in all the local newspapers and was thumbtacked to the wall in every police station. If he'd continued to commit his crimes, they would have caught him. Their theory was that he'd left the region. Shelby glanced back at the dates. His last appearance in Visalia dated back to December 1975—six months before the spate of rapes in Sacramento County started.

Chapter 5

If the Visalia Ransacker and the East Area Rapist were the same man, that only confirmed the Sacramento sheriff's department's theory about California in the 1960–70s. Their region was a magnet that attracted bloody killers, rapists, and sociopaths from all over the United States. Some of the cases were familiar to everyone, of course. Like Charles Manson, the Los Angeles guru with his wild black hair. People said he had the look of the devil. In 1969, he'd sent some of his adolescent disciples to kill actress Sharon Tate and her friends in a massacre that had a whiff of semi-satanic rite.

Or the Zodiac killer, the assassin who had committed five murders, according to the official count. For years, he had been taunting police and the local media, sending them letters after each crime, composed of cryptograms to decipher. He signed them with a circle and a cross that looked like crosshairs on a gun.

And there were others. Cases that operated outside the media spotlight, cases just as terrible and with just as many victims. The "Stinky Rapist," who smelled of gasoline and was responsible for dozens of rapes in Berkeley in the 1970s. The "California Pillowcase Rapist," who covered his victims' faces with a pillow. The "Sacramento Vampire," who killed his victims and drank their blood, then removed some of their organs to eat them.

How was it possible that California, this Eden of the American dream, this promise of love, sunlight, and a fresh start in life, had slipped into such horror? Sitting at the counter in Marie's Donuts or Pine Cove, places where they could decompress, the Sacramento police often concluded their nights with this question. And just as often, they went home without an answer.

Shelby had a feeling that the man he was tracking fit this gruesome category. What worried him most was that as the months passed, the perpetrator seemed to gain confidence. In the past, his invisibility had been one of his notable features. But now, when someone spotted him, he sometimes stood stock still for a couple of seconds, as if daring them to come after him. Then he'd start moving again—unruffled—and disappear.

Some witnesses even reported seeing him ride casually on a bicycle through the streets of Rancho Cordova in the middle of the night, wearing a ski mask. Another time, he brazenly chased after a woman on his bike, as she drove home in her car. She accelerated, trying to lose him, but he was relentless. Each time she lifted her foot off the gas, she said, she could see the dark blob gaining on her in the moonlight. Finally, he dropped away.

Like the Zodiac, who had amused himself by sending messages to the police and the media through the mail, the East Area Rapist took pleasure in taunting the Sacramento detectives. To one of his victims, he'd said, "You tell those fucking pigs that I could have killed two people tonight. If I don't see that all over the papers and television, I'll kill two people tomorrow night." That same day, *The Sacramento Bee* ran the headline "East Area Rapist Attacks No. 23 Next Victims Die Tonight?" A few hours later, officers were staggering under the flood of calls from frightened citizens.

On March 18, 1977, a husky male voice phoning into the sheriff's department said, "I'm the EAR," then laughed and hung up. It was 4:55 P.M. Fifteen minutes later, another call from a man at the same number repeated "I'm the EAR," then laughed and hung up. At 5:00 P.M., a third call: "I'm the East Area Rapist. I have my next victim already stalked, and you guys can't catch me." Again, he laughed and hung up. A few hours later, at 10:45 P.M., a sixteen-year-old girl was raped in Rancho Cordova. She was victim number fifteen.

The next day, *The Sacramento Bee* wrote that the rapist "only attacked women home alone or with their children." Perhaps this was meant to reassure women readers in the county by implying that if their husbands were there, they had nothing to fear. But apparently, to the rapist, it also felt like a slap in the face, implying that he wouldn't have the "courage" to take on a man.

Whatever the intent behind the comment, it was a mistake. From then on, almost every attack resulted in two direct victims.

On April 2, 1977, in Orangevale, a town east of Citrus Heights and near the American River, a young couple went to the evening show at the movies. Once back home, they put their two children to bed, and the husband hung out in the living room. A little before two in the morning, he went to bed. An hour later, his wife woke up to the glare of a flashlight in her face. A man with a raspy voice murmured, "Don't make a sound. See this gun? Wake up your husband." The young woman obeyed. The husband, also blinded by the light, tried to get up.

"Don't move. Turn over on your stomach. I have a .45 mm with two cartridges. Stay there, lying down, or I'll kill you."

Again, he pointed the flashlight at the woman and ordered her to tie up her husband with a pair of white shoelaces that he threw on the bed.

"And make it tight."

When she'd finished, the intruder, who was wearing a ski mask, tied her up and then left to search the house. The couple could hear sounds in the kitchen. When the intruder came back, he had a cup and saucer, which he balanced on the husband's back. He whispered the rules of the game.

"If I hear the dishes rattle or the bedsprings make noise, I'll shoot everybody in the house." Then he dragged the woman into the hallway, put spike heels on her feet, and raped her three times.

Two hours later, the perpetrator stuck his head in the bedroom, where the husband still lay on his stomach. "Next stop, another town." Then he disappeared.

That set off a new series of attacks. On April 15, there were two new victims in Carmichael. On May 3, the same thing happened on Riviera Drive, right in

Sacramento. Then on May 5 and 14 in Orangevale and Citrus Heights. Each time, he attacked a woman and her spouse.

On May 17, there was another call. This was the twenty-first rape victim. When Shelby and Daly arrived at her house, the husband answered the door. Shelby recognized him immediately. Six months earlier, they had met at a community meeting held at the Del Dayo Elementary School in Carmichael. For the second time, Shelby and Daly were there to warn the residents of the rapist who was prowling the region. A man had stood up and shouted angrily that in Italy, where he was born, the police and the public would already have caught the rapist and punished him. Now, the same man stood before them.

The two detectives wondered if the East Area Rapist had wanted to make an example of him, showing that he feared no one. Did this mean the rapist had been in the crowd at that November 4 meeting at the elementary school? Had their eyes met, and did the perpetrator know the faces of the cops who were pursuing him? Daly had a feeling the answer to all three questions was yes. But what she and her colleague didn't yet realize was that the East Area Rapist also knew Richard Shelby's home address.

Chapter 6

One night in May 1977, four-year-old Tom Shelby heard loud noises on the roof over his head. The footsteps sounded so heavy he thought they were going to break the roof. The little boy was scared. He looked around but didn't see anything. He looked out the window. There was a man right outside, his head upside down. He was looking into Tom's bedroom. The black ski mask he was wearing had a pom pom on it that bobbed back and forth. His flashlight lit up Tom's whole room. The long beam swept across the room, then snapped off. Tom saw the man's head go back up and disappear. Tom got out of bed and ran to his parents' bedroom. He climbed into their bed and fell back to sleep. His father, Richard Shelby, heard nothing.

The next morning, the little boy told him what had happened. He'd heard a man walking on the roof. He'd seen a man wearing a ski mask who lit up his bedroom with a flashlight. Shelby was petrified. He was sure the child could not have imagined all those details. Not the ski mask and the flashlight. He had no doubts about the intruder's identity. The East Area Rapist had paid him a visit. The investigator's normally square shoulders sagged. Who was hunting whom in this investigation?

Since May 17 of that year, when the serial rapist had whispered in his twenty-first victim's ear, "Those pigs, those fucking cops, I'm going to kill them too," the entire county police force was on alert. The perpetrator's appearance at Shelby's house confirmed what they all suspected: This man's insanity knew no bounds. After that, fellow officers stood guard outside Shelby's house when he went out on patrol at night. Inside the house, his wife Eleanor kept a gun within reach. She also had Squire, their German shepherd.

But Shelby felt weary. Every night, he knocked on doors, staked out houses, watched helicopters flying over the region like a war zone, positioned camouflaged cops in the dark undergrowth, and watched armed citizen groups take shape. All that for nothing. The sergeant had plunged into the case as deep as he possibly could yet remained stuck in a thick fog.

Despite corresponding features, he'd never been able to establish a concrete connection between the Visalia Ransacker and the East Area Rapist. Nor had he made any progress on establishing the serial rapist's identity. All he had were police sketches that led to nothing and a list of victims that kept growing. No progress, no movement, no cracks. And the East Area Rapist had now committed over twenty crimes.

On May 28, a young woman and her husband were attacked by a masked individual in South Sacramento. It was the last time Shelby set foot in one of the crime scenes. He was taken off the East Area Rapist investigation team and reassigned. His superiors realized he was exhausted and the investigation was not moving forward. His contentious relationship with the ranking officers in the department didn't help.

The detective took five weeks of R&R. He'd often heard his colleagues say that leaving a case meant leaving your obsessions and bad memories in the pages of your last police report. But not Shelby. The East Area Rapist case was a hell that continued to burn. He spent his entire "vacation" at home in Rancho Cordova, a bourbon on the rocks at hand. Sometimes he pressed the glass to his forehead, as if to cool down his brain.

He couldn't help but notice a coincidence of events: When he left the investigation, the East Area Rapist stopped attacking. But it only lasted two months, July and August. On September 6, another couple was attacked, this time in Stockton, a town about forty minutes from Sacramento. For the first time, the perpetrator had acted outside the county and struck farther to the south. Same MO as always. Then more attacks came on October 1, October 21, October 29, November 10, and December 2. The only detective who kept digging into the investigation each day was Carol Daly.

Chapter 7

Before integrating into the special task force to pursue the East Area Rapist, Carol Daly had been part of the team of detectives charged with investigating the Sacramento Vampire. It was a story that would make your blood run cold. The murderer, Richard Chase, drank his victims' blood and sometimes ate their brains. Yet throughout, Daly had never averted her eyes. Since her first day on the force, she'd looked straight at the horrors of her profession—rapes, murders, injuries—confident that she was in the right place. Flooding her vision with the evil out there was the right thing to do. That was her mission, and it was God who had so decided.

Carol Daly hadn't been born in a church, but it seemed like it. Raised in Kearney, a small burg in central

Nebraska, she'd spent her childhood at the presbytery, praying, playing the piano, and helping to organize mass, weddings, and other events connected with the local Catholic community. Her parents' house was surrounded on all sides by cornfields and farms. In her bedroom closet hung Carol's only dress, and she took good care of it. She rode her horses—Dick, Doc, Duke, and Dan—bareback. The town of Kearney was divided in two by railroad tracks that marked a clear border through the city. On the north side lived the upper-class families; on the south side, the less well-off. Daly was "a south side girl," but she didn't intend to be there forever.

In the 1960s, she set out for Sacramento, where she was one of the first women to join the sheriff's department. There were only eight women on the force at the time: Charlene Fowler, Carol Petty, Patty Butler, Shell Finley, Mona Kelsey, Joyce Pearson, Alex Cowan Magness, and Carol Daly. They were not allowed to wear pants, but they weren't given a women's uniform either. Such a thing didn't exist. The women were also prohibited from going out on patrols and were required to carry their pistols in their handbags. They underwent special training to learn how to draw their weapon from their purse as fast as men could draw theirs from the holsters on their belts.

When the case of the East Area Rapist erupted, it soon became clear that the department's handling of victims was disastrous. The male police officers had received no training for this kind of investigation. They interrupted a fifteen-year-old victim who was recounting her attack, saying, "We just want the facts, just give us the facts." What interested them was the size of the attacker's penis. The young girl had no idea. They pressed her. "Was it bigger or smaller than a hotdog? Or a pickle? Think!"

For many victims, these interrogations felt like a second violation. Officers questioned them a few yards from where they had been tied up just hours earlier. Sometimes a victim was just wrapped in a bath towel or bed sheet. The officers led victims from one room to another and photographed them.

Carol Daly was brought onto the investigation team, in part to correct the officers' approach. In addition, as the woman officer, she was put in charge of taking all victim statements at the crime scene. Her nights were transformed into periods of waiting. When the telephone rang, she had to be on the scene in under fifteen minutes. When she arrived, Daly immediately headed for the victim. She listened to her story, taking the victim's hands in hers. Sometimes she asked, "Would you like to pray? Pray with me?"

After questioning them, she drove the victims to the Sacramento Medical Center. Later in the evening, she sometimes returned there to take them a hot meal. When one of the victims, a teenager, celebrated her birthday a few days after her attack, Carol was waiting in front of her house with a gift when the young woman got home from school. Daly grew to be a faithful support. Three of the victims called her "Mom."

Daly was also the point person for the community information sessions. In a calm voice, she addressed the women in the room specifically, saying things like, "I would like to emphasize something, ladies. We have all been raised to be polite and avoid hurting people. Stop. [. . .] You've asked me, 'If we have a gun, can we shoot him?' From what I know about this man, I would not hesitate a second to shoot him if I had a gun, and I would not shoot to wound. I would shoot to get rid of him."

At home, Daly kept a gun on her nightstand. Her husband, Ted, also a police officer, kept another one next to his pillow. After the rapist openly threatened the investigators, the department insisted on installing a floor alarm in the Daly home. Placed inside the front door, it looked like a thick rug. It was wired directly to the police station and sent a "Code 3" alert—immediate intervention with rotating lights and sirens—if someone stepped on it. But they only kept the alarm for a few days. Daly's children and her dog kept stepping on it throughout the day, and she was tired of rushing to the phone each time it happened to stop the whole county police force from showing up at her door.

Yet Daly sensed that the worst was yet to come and affirmed that to women residents of the county. She had seen the offender evolve since the first attacks. The most recent victims told her that his voice was now trembling and stuttering, that he shouted, cried, grew upset, and cursed his mother in a corner of the bedroom. Increasingly often, he threatened to kill—the victims, witnesses, cops. Daly and her fellow officers on the task force braced themselves for the day when the perpetrator would convert his words into acts. He was already suspected of shooting an adolescent boy, who had chased after him after catching him prowling around his backyard the previous February. The perpetrator had shot him in the abdomen and had fired a second shot, with no hesitation. Psychologists warned, "He has a powerful need to kill."

On February 2, 1978, it finally happened. Brian, twenty-one years of age, and Katie, twenty, were out walking their silver poodle on the streets of Rancho Cordova. The Maggiores were a model couple. He had fine features; she had wavy, chestnut hair. At around 9:10 P.M., they turned onto La Alegria Drive, two blocks from their apartment. They greeted a neighbor—a policeman—then chased after their dog, which, for some strange reason, had suddenly run off into the backyard of a nearby house.

What happened then was told to the police by a ten-year-old child who lived next door and who watched the scene unfold from a distance. When the couple ran into the backyard, they found themselves face-to-face with a prowler. Based on where the bodies lay on the ground, police deduced that Brian had tried to make a break for the patio and was shot twice. Katie had tried to escape, running toward the fence. A bullet struck her in the head. Neighbors heard her scream. Marks on the walls showed that she had almost managed to get away. The neighbors, alerted by the commotion, rushed out to help and saw the attacker but were unable to stop him.

Brian and Katie, both seriously wounded, were taken to the university medical center in Sacramento. Brian died at 11:14 P.M. Katie died twenty minutes later.

In the yard where the couple had been assassinated, the police found white shoelaces on the ground. They had already been knotted and were ready to be slipped over wrists and jerked tight in a single, quick motion. A sketch artist drew a portrait of the murderer based on the testimony of the residents who'd gotten a look at him. The portrait showed a man with brown hair brushed to the right side. He had a square jaw, almond eyes, and a contemptuous grin. In the days that followed, the sketch was published in every press outlet in the county. He would never strike there again. Publishing his face silenced him, like the Visalia Ransacker before him.

However, he soon resurfaced farther north, closer to San Francisco, in Yolo, Stanislaus, Alameda, San Joaquin, and Contra Costa Counties. At least fifteen women were attacked in these five counties in a little over a year, from June 5, 1978, to July 6, 1979. Then nothing. This time forever. The series of attacks ended as mysteriously as it had begun. To use the attacker's own expression, he "was gone in the dark."

Carol Daly viewed the last crimes from afar. They had not taken place in her jurisdiction, and nobody had called her. She felt no offense. She was even relieved. Like Richard Shelby a year earlier, Daly felt drained by the enigma of the East Area Rapist, as well as the endless suffering he left in his wake. At night, when she closed her eyes, she now imagined being startled awake by the blinding glare of a flashlight. She avoided neighborhood parties and Sunday barbecues, knowing the guests would descend on her with endless questions about the case.

Worst of all, she just couldn't absorb the testimonies like she used to, using God as a shoulder to lean on. She couldn't tolerate hearing herself tell victims that the investigation had ground to a halt, even after scrutinizing a list of some five thousand suspects and after analyzing the profiles of dozens of men of interest. So, a few months after the East Area Rapist disappeared from Sacramento County, Carol Daly walked into her supervisor's office and requested a transfer to homicide, where she had worked for several years previously. Her supervisor raised an eyebrow.

"You know that it's just as hard in homicide?"

"Yes," she answered, "but at least when I was there, we shed light on ninety-eight percent of the cases. We solved murders. At some point, we solved them all."

II CONNECTIONS 1980–2018

Chapter 8

Roger Harrington, aged sixty-three, did not want to live in this house in Dana Point, a coastal town less than an hour from Los Angeles. It had all kinds of pluses—its southern exposure and the view overlooking the Pacific; the beach a short walk away; and the décor with its white walls, lots of natural wood, a mounted swordfish trophy, and a Tiffany chandelier—the whole thing communicated social success. But Harrington, who had made a fortune in the video surveillance business, had always said it was too far from the action. He preferred his Lakewood apartment farther north, close to his office. So recently, he'd left the house to his newly married son Keith, aged twenty-four, and daughter-in-law Patrice, or Patti, aged twenty-seven.

On August 21, 1980, at 6:30 P.M., Roger Harrington arrived at 33381 Cockleshell Drive to have dinner with the young couple. On the mailbox out front, he found a message left by Patti's friends, which read "We came by at 7:00 P.M., but no one was home. Call us if plans have changed." There were a dozen letters in the mailbox. Puzzled, Harrington gave the front door a shove. It was locked. But they always left the house open. He reached up and grabbed the key that his son kept hidden atop the doorframe.

Inside the house, he was met with darkness and a deathly silence. A bag of groceries was sitting on the kitchen counter next to the sink. Three slices of sandwich bread left on the table were stale. Harrington felt his stomach turn. He checked all the rooms, one by one, until he reached the master bedroom. In the dark, he could make out a lump under the sheets. Roger approached and pulled back the sheet. Keith lay there on his stomach. His face, turned to the left, was bloody. Patrice lay next to him, also on her stomach. She was dead. Her face was unrecognizable. They both had visible marks on their wrists and ankles from ligatures. They had been tied up before being killed.

The autopsy revealed that the couple had been dead for two days. There was no sign of forced entry. Patti had been raped several times. The investigators found sperm inside her, on her back, and on the quilt. The young couple had died of blunt force trauma to the head with a "blunt instrument." The amount of force used was shocking to every person who read the report. The killer had covered his victims' faces with the bedspread before slaughtering them. A lieutenant summarized the situation in the August 23 issue of the *Los Angeles Times*. "This case is a mystery for us." Indeed, the Harrington family announced an award of $25,000 in September for any information leading to the arrest of the murderer. But no one responded.

Six months later, on February 6, 1981, Manuela Witthuhn, a woman twenty-eight years of age, was found murdered in Irvine, about twenty minutes from Dana Point and the Harrington residence. David and Manuela Witthuhn had lived in the two-story house for a little more than a year. On the night of the crime, David was at the Santa Ana-Tustin Community Hospital for a viral infection. Manuela was home alone. She was raped, then bludgeoned to death. Some ten detectives were assigned to the case. Despite the similarities with the murders in Dana Point, no connection could be established between the Harrington case and the Witthuhn case. No suspect was arrested either.

Fifteen years went by. Fifteen long years during which neither the police nor the Harrington family nor the Witthuhn family found any answers. It was not until December 1995 that the sheriff's department in Orange County, where Dana Point and Irvine are located, decided to blow the dust off these cold cases and submit them to DNA testing. Even though the development of DNA fingerprinting, which allows the determination of a unique genetic identity for each individual, dated from 1985, and even though the technology had already been used in a number of investigations, its more widespread use was quite recent. The DNA Identification Act, which allowed the FBI to create a national database, had only been enacted one year earlier, in 1994. Since then, all criminals whose DNA had been taken were entered into a huge electronic registry, which gave impetus to reopen old cases.

The county criminal analysis laboratory analyzed the traces of sperm found in the Harrington and Witthuhn cases. No name came up. That was a disappointment, but the tests did yield other information. The genetic fingerprints in these two cases were the same, which meant the same man was responsible for all three murders. While the goal of these new investigations was to close dozens of old cases, here it had the opposite effect. A few weeks after the connection was established between the Harrington and Witthuhn murders, the file grew fatter with a third case: the murder of Janelle Cruz, eighteen years old.

A real estate agent had found Janelle's body in her mother's house, which was up for sale and located only a few minutes by foot from the home of Manuela Witthuhn. The murder took place on May 5, 1986, five years after the Witthuhn murder. Janelle Cruz was found lying diagonally across her bed, her bra pulled down to her waist. Her face had been bludgeoned with such force that she had swallowed a tooth. The blows had projected two other teeth into her hair.

Cruz had spent her last hours with a friend, a young man. They had been in her room, talking. Cruz had read him a few of her own poems, then played the recording of a session with her psychologist. The friend reported to the investigators that twice during their conversations, they'd heard sounds coming from outside, near their house. The first time, the sounds came from outside her bedroom window. The second time, from the yard. It sounded like someone jumping over the fence. Both times, Janelle and her friend looked out the window but saw nothing suspicious. The friend left Cruz at 10:45 P.M. A few hours later, Janelle Cruz was dead.

Three crime scenes and one criminal. The Orange County Sheriff's Department began to worry that a serial killer had been operating with impunity all these years. The man's DNA profile was sent to various criminal laboratories around the country. They were looking for unsolved crimes from ten, fifteen, even twenty years before.

In February 1998, they got a bite elsewhere in California. The case dated from March 13, 1980, and the crime had taken place north of Los Angeles, in Ventura. A couple was murdered in their house in the middle of the night, bludgeoned to death with a piece of firewood. Their names were Lyman Smith, aged forty-three, and Charlene Smith, aged thirty-three. The woman had been raped. The sperm recovered at the crime scene is what had allowed investigators to link this double homicide to the earlier ones.

After that, two more cases showed parallels: two couples in Santa Barbara County, massacred in similar conditions, in 1979 and 1981. No trace of DNA had been found at the crime scenes, but the MO was so similar that the investigators were convinced the same man was behind these murders.

Totaling up the crimes was dizzying. Between 1979 and 1986, a serial killer murdered ten people on the California coast without anyone connecting the crimes. On October 1, 2000, the local newspaper, *The Orange County Register*, carried a large headline that read "Serial Killer Revealed by His DNA." As usual, the American press soon bestowed a moniker on the killer: the "Original Night Stalker."

It would take another six months for the investigation to make any progress. In April 2001, forty-three-year-old Paul Holes, a zealous criminologist in the forensics department of the Contra Costa County Sheriff's Department, decided to compare the murderer's DNA to that of the East Area Rapist, which had been collected in the rape kits of three victims in Sacramento County.

Fascinated by this rapist case, Holes was convinced that these two offenders were actually the same. The MOs in the crimes committed in Northern, then Southern

California seemed too similar not to be acts committed by the same person. He was correct. When the test results came back, they were conclusive. The East Area Rapist was also the Original Night Stalker. He was a rapist and a killer.

The Sacramento investigators had long wondered why this offender, who had attacked women who were home alone, then couples, had abruptly ceased his activity after July 6, 1979. Now they understood that the perpetrator had never stopped—he'd just migrated a few hours down the road toward the south. There, his threats of murder had escalated into acts, as Richard Shelby and Carol Daly had suspected.

Still unanswered was the question of the five-year hiatus between the murders of the Domingo-Sanchez couple in 1981 and Janelle Cruz in 1986. Another question: Why nothing after 1986? The laboratories were categorical. No other attack inventoried beyond that date had been linked to the murderer's DNA. The most logical hypothesis was that the serial killer-rapist had been convicted of other crimes since then and was incarcerated somewhere in the state. So, they started comparing his DNA to that of the fifty thousand detainees being held in California prisons. The task was daunting and yielded inconclusive results. Maybe the perpetrator had moved out of state? Or maybe he'd died? That was probably the most likely explanation for his silence and disappearance.

However, the worst was always yet to come with the East Area Rapist. On April 6, 2001, two days after the newspapers confirmed that the serial rapist was also responsible for ten murders in southern California, a previous victim in Sacramento received a telephone call. She heard a sigh before a deep, gravelly voice spoke. The victim recognized it immediately, even decades later. The voice of the man who had attacked her on the night of March 8, 1977. He rasped, "Remember when we played?"

Chapter 9

On April 21, 2016, in Los Angeles, a woman named Michelle McNamara swallowed a cocktail of medications, including Adderall, Xanax, and fentanyl. The dose was fatal. While sorting through her belongings in the days after her death, her family found 3,500 files on her computer, in addition to thirty-seven cardboard boxes crammed with papers, lists, thousands of pages of notes, and, buried in this mountain of information, a document titled, "Letter to an old man."

In the letter, Michelle McNamara had written, "After May 4, 1986, you disappeared. Some think you died. Others think you are in prison. Not me. I think you bailed when the world began to change. Technology is progressing. You cut out when you looked over your shoulder and saw your opponents gaining on you. One day soon, you'll hear a car pull up to your curb, an engine cut out. You'll hear footsteps coming up your front walk [. . .]. The doorbell rings. Take one of your hyper, gulping breaths. Clench your teeth. Inch timidly toward the insistent bell. This is how it ends for you. 'You'll be silent forever, and I'll be gone in the dark,' you threatened a victim once. Open the door. Show us your face. Walk into the light."

Michelle McNamara had become obsessed with the East Area Rapist in 2010 after reading *Sudden Terror*, the novel that Larry Crompton, a former Contra Costa investigator, had dedicated to the case. She was gripped by the story. How was it possible that one of the worst criminals of the last decades had never been identified? And why had it remained just a local news story? The Zodiac, Ted Bundy, Edmund Kemper—they were serial killers known all over the world. Books and university theses had been written on them. Films, both fiction and documentaries, had focused on them. But from the beginning, the aura of the East Area Rapist had not spread beyond the wooded areas of Sacramento County. The only book dedicated to it was gathering dust on the back shelves of used bookstores, and the media outlets that used the EAR's crimes for headlines were obscure: *The Sacramento Bee* and *The Orange County Register.*

The greatest share of information could be found on the internet, where crime story enthusiasts of all kinds exchanged information in forums. Michelle McNamara dove in. She read thousands of comments dedicated to the serial rapist and murderer and became saturated with unanswered questions and possible leads. She filled dozens of yellow legal pads with scribbled notes retracing the complete progression of the East Area Rapist. She got to know the neighborhoods in Rancho Cordova, Citrus Heights, and Carmichael, the sinuous streets and the unpaved paths shaded by oak trees. She located each victim's house and tried to discern some kind of hidden significance in the perpetrator's choice of crime scenes.

In a few years, Michelle McNamara had acquired such a depth of knowledge regarding the case that she felt on equal footing with the police. She had even formed a sort of friendship with some of them. She'd met Larry Crompton, a detective in the Contra Costa sheriff's department, and Larry Pool, an Orange County detective. For a long time, she exchanged emails with Richard Shelby. She also grew closer to Paul Holes, chief of forensics in Contra Costa. Together, they compared leads and drove around San Ramon, Danville, Davis, and Concord, tracking the serial killer's progression until they could do it with their eyes closed.

In 2013, Michelle McNamara published a feature article in the *Los Angeles Magazine*, which told the story of her hunt for the East Area Rapist, detailing all she'd learned about the perpetrator and his crimes. Her avowed goal was to lay everything out for the media as a way to reopen the investigation, which, until then, had been limited to work by a handful of police officers who had to do most of their investigating in their free time.

She was clear-eyed, realizing that marketing also counted when it came to serial rapists. Would Jack the Ripper have been so famous with a less catchy nickname? The killers themselves had learned this lesson. For example, Zodiac had given himself that name. In the case of the Sacramento County killer, they weren't sure who they were dealing with. He had two sobriquets, the East Area Rapist and the Original Night Stalker. McNamara was convinced he needed a new name, and in her article, she decided to take care of that matter herself. From then on, he would be known as the "Golden State Killer."

To all appearances, Michelle McNamara had no particular reason to hunt down a serial rapist. She knew none of the victims and had no connection to Northern

California. But she did have an account to settle with unsolved crimes. On August 1, 1984, when Michelle was fourteen, the body of Kathleen Lombardo had been found in Oak Park, Illinois, her throat slit while she was out jogging. At the time, McNamara lived in Oak Park too.

Several days after the murder, she'd gone to the crime scene. There, she saw pieces of Kathleen's broken Walkman on the ground. She gathered them up and took them home with her. The young jogger's murderer was never found. In the years that followed, Michelle moved out to Hollywood, where she became a screenwriter and met her husband, the actor Patton Oswalt. But more than fiction, it was cold cases that became McNamara's fight. She knew them inside and out. In 2006, she even created a website, truecrimediary.com, which attempted to solve old cases. To people close to her, she confirmed that she wasn't motivated by a desire for glory or the thrill of unraveling a mystery that others had failed to solve, but rather, she was seeking justice. Because those men should be in jail.

Of all the cases she examined, the one McNamara called the Golden State Killer became her top priority. She spent entire days pursuing new leads. For example, at one point, she had the idea of comparing all the names of those buried in the Goleta cemetery to the list of alumni from schools in Irvine—two towns where the murderer had struck—hoping that some name would connect the two.

Another time, she spent an afternoon bogged down investigating a member of a water polo team from 1972 at Rio Americano High School in Sacramento because, like the Golden State Killer, he was a thin man with large calf muscles. She also developed an exhaustive list of the items stolen by the perpetrator during his expeditions. She spent entire hours searching online marketplace sites, waiting for one of the stolen items to reappear.

Michelle McNamara knew only too well the stories of investigators who had sacrificed their family life or their lives with a partner to this investigation. She knew some of them had gone under, and she knew she was gradually falling into the same trap. The more her research progressed, the more trouble she had sleeping. At night, she panicked at the slightest sound: a neighbor setting out trash cans, her husband getting ready for work. Sometimes she felt compelled to get up in the middle of the night to check a question that had just occurred to her.

There were mornings when her husband found her at dawn hunched over her computer and crying tears of frustration because one of her leads had led to nothing.

She said she had a "scream permanently lodged in her throat." She began to take tranquilizers in secret, then increased the doses until the day she didn't wake up.

For Michelle McNamara, the Golden State Killer would forever remain a blurred face. *I'll Be Gone in the Dark*, the book she was writing on the investigation, was published posthumously on February 27, 2018. One of its theses was that the key to the perpetrator's identity lay in the genealogical sites that had begun to proliferate in the United States. What was required, she explained, was to compare the serial rapist's DNA to the tens of millions of profiles on those sites. A name would emerge.

Chapter 10

Analyze DNA fingerprints until an identity finally emerges. That same thought also obsessed Sergeant Detective Ken Clark in the early years of the twenty-first century. Clark had grown up in Sacramento during the era of the Golden State Killer's crimes. He was eight years old in 1976 when the rapist began terrorizing his county.

As a child, he had awakened nearly every morning to hear that a new victim had just been attacked. He'd seen the doors and the windows of his neighborhood closed and bolted. He'd watched fear, anger, and incomprehension gradually tighten their grip on the world of the adults who surrounded him. Much later, he started working in the Sacramento County Sheriff's Office, still haunted by this case. Assigned to Homicide in 2005, he decided the time had come to dive into this case.

At the time, his unit consisted of only eight detectives who were responsible for solving sixty crimes a year. Criminal statistics had exploded over the years, thanks to drugs and gangs, which now flooded the region. Clark was overwhelmed, but that didn't lessen the importance of this twenty-nine-year-old case. For him, it was inconceivable that despite knowing a single perpetrator was responsible for ten murders in the southern part of the state, a reservist was the only person still studying police reports relating to the East Area Rapist. The department had seemingly abandoned the investigation, without admitting it, for lack of time, funding, or progress. So, Clark took the files home to begin reading them. After Richard Shelby, after Carol Daly, he prepared to add his own name to the list of investigators who had been devoured by the case.

Ken Clark hoped a fresh pair of eyes would see new elements emerge. But he could discern nothing that hadn't already been checked out once, twice, ten times, a hundred times. And yet he persisted, convinced that the rapist-murderer was still out there, alive. He felt sure that the perpetrator was still living in the area as the Everyman on one of those suburban streets.

Clark took up the list of the five thousand people who had been suspects at one point or another: burglars, sexual deviants, prowlers, plus ordinary citizens with clean records who found their way on the list through an angry ex-wife or spiteful neighbor. Convicted criminals or not, the vast majority had never submitted their DNA, and many had disappeared from circulation.

Clark faced a mountain of work that would take years to climb. He dug in. Approaching unknown people to ask for a sample of their saliva was out of the question. Instead, the detective found other ways to gather samples, by picking up a cigarette butt thrown on the ground and digging beer or soda cans out of the trash after the suspect had carelessly tossed them there. Alongside this effort, he worked up a list of about one hundred people he considered the most likely suspects scattered around the country and requested the support of the FBI. DNA samples started flowing into the Sacramento crime laboratory. Not a single lead. That was a real setback.

Next, Clark reexamined the thirty thousand police reports coming out of Sacramento County in 1973, the year before Visalia was ravaged by a burglar-turned-killer. Like Richard Shelby before him, Clark was convinced the East Area Rapist and Visalia Ransacker were the same man. He was trying to find out if that man had operated in Sacramento County before fleeing to Tulare County.

In the archives, he read through a parade of microform slides, one at a time, on the heavy, outdated gray readers, technology from an earlier era. The images were often of poor quality, with the edges cut off; sometimes they were even upside down. It took Clark four months to read through all the files for the year. No new suspects, but he did discover that in early 1973, Rancho Cordova had experienced a series of burglaries. An intruder who shared the East Area Rapist's MO and was in the same area, but three years later. At the time, he had been dubbed the Cordova Cat Burglar. One of his victims would also become an East Area Rapist victim in 1976. Clark dove into the files for 1976, 1977, and 1978. Tens of thousands more reports.

How about going back to speak to the police officers from those years? It wasn't hard to convince Shelby. The former cop was now over seventy, his hair thinner, and his posture was more rounded than when he'd retired. He had left the department in 1993 with the rank of lieutenant.

Until the day he retired, he'd continued to follow up on leads on his own, as always. He kept an eye on the suspects he'd been following for years. When DNA research became accessible, he had no compunction about diving into a suspect's trash to unearth a sample of his DNA. Three times he'd done it. On another occasion, he'd followed a suspect into a restaurant, where he asked the server not to clear the table. Shelby took one of the eating utensils used by the suspect. But none of these men had DNA identical to that of the East Area Rapist.

When Ken Clark showed Shelby his findings regarding 1973, Shelby recounted his memories of that year. The dogs killed, the man on the roof. The Cordova Cat Burglar. He helped Clark with the reports from 1976 and 1977, guiding him on leads that he'd been unable to follow and names of suspects he'd been unable to track down. And he wasn't the only one to do that. Clark was part of a new task force, launched in 2011, that included the top brass among the investigators obsessed with the case of the serial killer. Detectives Greg and Russ Hayes, a father and son from Ventura County, Inspector Larry Pool from Santa Barbara County, and Paul Holes, chief of the Contra Costa County forensics department, the one who had established the link between the rapes in Northern California to the murders in the southern part of the state.

They all agreed with the assessment of Michelle McNamara, with whom they sometimes spoke, that

DNA was the key to this case. Paul Holes was most adamant of all on this point since learning in 2017 that a San Bernardino detective had managed to identify a young girl whose body had been found at an abandoned campsite way back in 1996. He'd used a website developed for people adopted as small children and used their DNA to trace their origins.

Learning about this case in 2017 gave Holes the idea of doing the same to establish the identity of the Golden State Killer. Holes tried sites like ancestry.com and 23andMe.com, associations which, in exchange for a saliva sample and just under one hundred dollars, would provide analysis of your DNA and inform you of your origins. Millions of people had turned to them to confirm family history or locate distant relatives. With a little luck, Holes thought, some relative of the Golden State Killer had submitted a sample.

Armed with those results, they would be able to trace the lineage to the perpetrator. Thanks to sperm residue retrieved from a crime scene, Holes was able to upload the criminal's genetic fingerprint to the FamilyTreeDNA.com and GEDMatch.com sites. He compared them to several millions of people and received a list of distant relatives of the killer, third cousins, for example. A family of several thousand people.

Then, in February 2018, a genealogist named Barbara Rae Venter, who was working with Paul Holes, sent him an email message: "I think we just got a hit." She had uploaded the Golden State Killer's DNA profile to another site called MyHeritage.com. This time, the results included the names of distant cousins. In a few weeks, the investigators had listed a dozen possible relatives of the killer, or, indeed, perhaps the killer himself. Then they investigated each of the profiles. The first was quickly eliminated because his sister's DNA did not correspond to that of the serial killer. Therefore, he was too distant.

The second suspect raised more flags. He was a former police officer who had served on the force in California in the 1970s. Born on November 8, 1945, he was five feet, ten inches tall with blue eyes. Clark compared the photos to the various police sketches of the criminal drawn over the years and saw one face. And this man was still alive. He was even still living there, right down the road in Sacramento County. At 8316 Canyon Oak Drive in Citrus Heights, to be exact. Just a few minutes' drive from former victims.

His name was Joseph DeAngelo.

Chapter 11

Ken Clark chose a black Toyota Camry for staking out the address. The Camry was one of the most widely sold cars in the United States and, therefore, the best for discreet stakeouts. On April 19, 2018, the police officer was resting his elbow on the edge of the window. He'd been operating on this new routine for several nights, arriving at about 7:00 P.M. and leaving at around 7:00 A.M. Twelve hours at a clip, doing nothing but staring straight ahead. Nearby, other unmarked cars had locked down the neighborhood. Better to err on the side of caution. If the suspect tried to move, he wouldn't get far.

The subject Clark was surveilling lived with one of his three daughters and her child. Joseph DeAngelo was seventy-two years old, of course, but to see him mow the lawn, it was clear that he had the energy of a younger man. The subject had gone out the previous day. The daytime surveillance team had tailed him to Hobby Lobby in Sacramento. While DeAngelo was in the store, they ran over to his car and wiped down the door handle to collect his DNA so his identity could be confirmed. The verdict of the laboratory analyses hadn't been delivered yet. Even though Clark had little doubt about the results, he remained skeptical. This would not be the first suspect to be found to be innocent.

The answer dropped on April 20. The resident living at 8316 Canyon Oak Drive was the Golden State Killer.

However, it was still too early to celebrate. Before going public with the information, Anne Marie Schubert, district attorney for Sacramento County, said she would need to see a second DNA sample. On April 21, at around 6:00 P.M., Clark was headed toward Citrus Heights a little ahead of schedule when a member of the stakeout team radioed the others to report the serial killer had just gotten into his car. A dozen officers in the area also turned on their ignition. Trailing DeAngelo from a short distance, they followed him through the narrow streets of Citrus Heights and onto the busy

Dwight D. Eisenhower Highway. Clark was about five minutes from his colleagues.

Suddenly, one of the officers alerted the team that the suspect seemed to be heading for Sacramento International Airport. Clark felt sweat trickle down his back. He wondered if the suspect had spotted them. It would take only one tiny thing—a neighbor noticing an unfamiliar Camry driving around the neighborhood or a glance exchanged with a detective—for Joseph DeAngelo to realize he was being surveilled and try to flee.

Once on the interstate, the DeAngelo vehicle accelerated. The Golden State Killer switched from the left lane to the right, as if attempting to expose a dragnet. The six unmarked vehicles of the investigators maintained their distance. A few minutes into this little game, there was no longer any doubt that the suspect was headed for the airport. Clark accelerated. He knew surveillance helicopters weren't allowed to fly over the airport zone and figured the killer, a former cop, knew it too. And that was exactly why he was heading in that direction.

As the secret race-pursuit continued on the freeway, the killer suddenly veered off onto an exit leading to the last service station before the airport. The six cars trailing him had no choice but to keep going for fear of being spotted. By chance, Clark was still trailing farther behind. He pulled into the parking lot a few minutes after the suspect. The sergeant spotted the suspect's vehicle. Joseph DeAngelo was still sitting in his car, not moving.

Clark parked a fair distance away and pulled out his binoculars. DeAngelo was alert, looking all around. He seemed to be braced for something. Maybe cars or faces that he'd seen near his home or in his rearview mirror on the highway. Maybe he was expecting a dozen officers to surround his vehicle, guns drawn, and order him to get out of the car. Twenty minutes later, he started the engine again. He drove through the airport, then back onto the freeway. Clark followed him the whole way at a distance. The Golden State Killer returned home to Citrus Heights.

Two days later, on April 23, the opportunity to collect a second DNA sample finally presented itself. The suspect had just taken his trash cans down to the curb. After night fell, the police officers fished out drink cans, bottles, and anything that might have touched his mouth.

Later that night, while waiting for the lab results, Paul Holes and Ken Clark wrote up the arrest warrant for the Golden State Killer. They listed his crimes and described his modus operandi. The document was a hundred pages long. "Between April 1974 and May

1986," it read, "a white man, hereafter referred to as the East Area Rapist, committed no less than 57 attacks that included sexual assaults and an additional thirteen homicides throughout California. He was responsible for hundreds of sexually motivated burglaries [. . .] and hang-up/lewd phone calls. The suspect in this series has now been identified by DNA. . ."

They requested his arrest for the murders of Brian and Katie Maggiore, the couple shot to death in a backyard. A double murder connected with the prosecutor's county. The rapes were beyond the statute of limitations.

The next day, the DNA sample collected from the items in the trash cans confirmed the killer's identity. Clark rushed to the prosecutor's office to get a judge to sign the warrant. The minutes that the magistrate took to read through the filing felt like hours. Clark fidgeted in his chair. He knew the arrest team would not budge until the warrant had been signed. After pausing, the judge took up his pen and finally added his signature.

Normally, the killer's home was a twenty-minute drive from the district attorney's office, but at this time of day, traffic was heavy. When Clark was finally approaching 8316 Canyon Oak Drive in Citrus Heights, he pulled over and jumped into a van parked near the corner grocery. At that moment, a voice on the police radio announced, "The suspect just stepped out of his house." The moment had finally arrived. After forty-two years, thirteen murders, some fifty rapes, and nearly two hundred burglaries, the Golden State Killer would finally be arrested.

Chapter 12

Ken Clark walked up the driveway slowly. Two more steps, then one, and he found himself face-to-face with Joseph DeAngelo. The serial killer was surrounded by a half dozen officers on the SWAT team and Fugitive Unit—officers specialized in the apprehension of dangerous criminals. DeAngelo was squealing, "What the fuck is going on?" If Clark had needed any more proof, he now had it. He recognized the voice that rose to a high pitch whenever the owner lost his cool. This was the voice described by so many victims. DeAngelo was handcuffed by an officer and then led to the back of the unmarked van.

Clark got into the front seat on the passenger side. He had been waiting for this moment for so long and suddenly realized he wasn't prepared. Should he say something? Nothing? Hope for a confession? He turned on a Dictaphone to record everything that might be said in the vehicle. But an unexpected silence took over the vehicle. DeAngelo was breathing fast and hard. Maybe he was assessing the scene, calculating his chances of getting out of this, or trying to figure out how much these investigators knew about: one crime, two crimes, dozens of crimes? Suddenly, he uttered a comment that threw everyone off. "I have a roast in the oven."

Clark shrugged. They would take care of it. He told the driver to start the van.

DeAngelo broke the silence only one other time during the drive to the Centralized Investigations Division, the building that had replaced the old sheriff's department and where so many cops had tried and failed to apprehend him all these years. "My handcuffs are too tight," he complained, looking up into the rearview mirror, where Clark's eyes were riveted on him.

Silence accompanied them into the interrogation room, which contained one metal table and two chairs. DeAngelo and Clark sat down on either each side of the table. A video camera mounted on the wall was filming the scene and transmitting the images onto a screen in an adjacent room. There, several detectives from other counties, plus Sacramento District Attorney Anne Marie Schubert, had all squeezed in. Schubert felt like she was looking at Hannibal Lecter in the flesh.

Ken Clark began. He explained to Joseph DeAngelo why he was there: that he stood accused of being the Golden State Killer and the author of at least fifty rapes, thirteen murders, and more than a hundred burglaries. His DNA linked him to the murders. Everything was there. Handcuffs off, sitting up straight on his chair, the accused didn't blink. The officer continued, describing the first rape case from June 1976. No reaction. Clark continued with the murders of Brian and Katie Maggiore. He referred to testimony by neighbors, conclusions of the police. Clark tried to arouse DeAngelo's curiosity with a few suggestive details.

He encouraged him, saying, "We can talk about this, if you want." He questioned him about the location, the murder, and his motives. But Joseph DeAngelo remained silent. "Catatonic" was the sergeant's term when he came out of the interrogation room.

Clark tried everything. He was by turns nice, close, open, calculating, authoritarian, distant—then all at the same time, with no success. In the course of his career, he'd conducted over two hundred interrogations. He had watched criminals break down in front of him, glare at him like they'd make him their next victim, even mock him. He'd seen all kinds of murderers, rapists, and psychopaths. Most of them started talking at some point. Not this one. After several hours, Clark turned him over to someone else to let the investigators from the other counties try their luck.

One of them brought DeAngelo a can of Dr Pepper. No reaction. Another one spread photographs of his crimes out on the table in front of him. No reaction. A third offered him a bathroom break. No answer. For eight hours, Joseph DeAngelo remained silent, sitting on his black chair. Not once did he react to the detectives' attempts. Not once did he speak—with one exception. When they left him alone in the interrogation room for a brief time, the microphones and camera recorded him muttering clipped sentences to himself. It was hard to make them out but worth the trouble.

"I didn't do anything," DeAngelo said to himself. "I took control. I grew stronger. I grew stronger. Finally, I took control. I made him leave. [. . .] I pushed Jerry out of my life. After that, my life was happy. So happy. Oh, it was so wonderful, it was wonderful, it was so wonderful. He was there all the time. [. . .] It was, like, in my head, I mean, he's a part of me. I didn't have the strength to push him out [. . .] I couldn't. I didn't want to go out,

I didn't want to do those things. He made me do it. I wasn't strong enough to fight. [. . .] My children are all suffering, they are suffering terribly, it's all so terrible because I was too weak."

A detective tried to seize this opportunity to make DeAngelo cave by leading the serial killer's daughters to the doorway of the interrogation room. DeAngelo stared at them silently. One of the daughters sobbed and said, "I love you, Dad." No reaction. Then, in a distant voice, he uttered, "Go away, go, go. Goodbye," repeating himself as if on a loop, even after the door had closed again.

The next day, Detective Clark went to Joseph DeAngelo's residence on Canyon Oak Drive. Investigators had been performing a meticulous search since the previous evening. Forbidding black-and-yellow tape marked SHERIFF'S LINE—DO NOT CROSS, and a half dozen police cars and FBI vehicles out front designated the crime scene, with a steady stream of agents coming and going between the house and their vehicles. They'd walk out with their arms full of boxes and objects wrapped in white plastic, then go back in for more. They recovered all the firearms belonging to the accused. They dug up the entire backyard. They went over it with a metal detector to uncover possible "souvenirs" taken from victims, which the accused might have buried.

They followed the same procedure on the walls inside the house and in the attic.

When Clark slipped inside for a look, he did not feel like he was entering a den of evil. It looked like the typical interior of the house of a middle-class grandfather. DeAngelo's bedroom was a monstrous pigsty, having already been turned upside down by the police. On a dresser near the bed, he noticed a photograph of the accused's mother. In the walk-in closet, he saw a jar of peanut butter. His eyes rested for a moment on the unmade bed, then on the computer. The towel draped over the monitor recalled the rapist's obsession with hanging towels over his victims' lit television screens. His taste for dim light.

DeAngelo's daughter and granddaughter were not in the house. They were in a state of shock, like the rest of his family. DeAngelo's sister Rebecca "didn't want to believe it." She had never seen anything at "Joe's" house to make her think he could do "things like that." Sharon, his ex-wife and the mother of his three daughters, made a short statement: "My thoughts and prayers are for the victims and their families." The investigators advised them all to cut their social bonds and warned them that a media tsunami was about to hit. Then they turned away to make more phone calls.

Chapter 13

.

Carol Daly was in the car when she received a call from the sheriff. His voice rang out in the car speakers.

"Hi, Carol, just wanted to notify you that we've identified the East Area Rapist."

"Are you kidding me?"

"Not really. His name is Joseph DeAngelo, and he's currently being held in custody."

The former officer, now seventy-eight years old, had never heard this name and didn't think she'd ever seen it on the suspect lists. But instead of wanting to dive back into the files to see if this information could shed new light on the case, her first instinct was to focus on the victims. She asked for some time to call the ones whose contact information she still had before the press had a chance to publish news of the breakthrough. Granted.

It was a race against the clock. Daly had dozens of calls to make and a window of only a few hours. Jane, the serial rapist's fifth victim, was the first person she reached. They had stayed in touch since 1976. She had intended to say, "Hey, Jane, we caught the East Area Rapist. He's in prison. Get ready," but their conversation was soon drowned out by a wave of shouts, tears, and questions.

Kris MacFarlane, now Kris Pedretti at fifty-seven years old, was in Los Angeles attending an American Cancer Society conference. When her cell phone pinged at around 6:00 A.M. on April 25, she was still in bed. A text message from her daughter read, "I think they caught him." She had just finished reading these mystifying words when her phone rang. It was Carol Daly. In a solemn tone, she said, "Kris, I have some news for you. They caught the East Area Rapist."

Kris MacFarlane doesn't remember what happened after that. She knows the sheriff also called, and then Steve, her husband. He said he was coming to pick her up. She told him that he didn't need to, and she took the first Southwest flight to Sacramento. It was a ninety-minute flight, and she cried the whole way in the last row of the plane. Over the years, she had convinced herself that her rapist was long dead. When she landed in Sacramento, she watched District Attorney Schubert give a press conference in which she declared, "Today is National DNA Day. [. . .] We have found the needle in the haystack. And it was right here in Sacramento."

Two days later, together with other victims and their families, Kris was led into a hearing room near the Sacramento County Supreme Court. She was seated in the first row with her husband, Steve. To her left in the same row sat Anne Marie Schubert. A dozen TV cameras from the media were lined up, waiting to capture their reactions to the defendant's arrival.

Finally, a door at the back of the room swung open. Kris saw Joseph DeAngelo appear in the doorway, surrounded by several officers. He was dressed in an orange prison jumpsuit and shackled to the wheelchair in which he was seated. His eyes were half-closed. He looked haggard, his jaw slack. The man who, days earlier, had been riding a motorcycle and mowing his lawn with the energy of a young man now appeared old. It wasn't clear if this was an act. Thick scabs were visible on his skull, as if he had been scratching his head in a frenzy. Paige St. John, a journalist from the *Los Angeles Times*, would later report, citing a "police source," that DeAngelo had been scraping his skull against the bars of his cell the night before.

The security officers settled Joe DeAngelo in his place facing the judge's rostrum, his back to the public. He was prohibited from looking at or speaking to the women behind him. Judge Michael Sweet leaned forward. "Is your name Joseph DeAngelo?" The "yes" uttered by DeAngelo, as his only response, was so muted that the judge had to ask him to repeat it. The prisoner was informed that he was being charged with the murders of Brian and Katie Maggiore and that he was being held in custody without bail. The judge asked DeAngelo if he had a lawyer with him. In a muted voice, Joseph DeAngelo answered, "I have a lawyer." Then the hearing was over.

DeAngelo was pushed toward the exit in his wheelchair. In all, the arraignment had lasted three minutes and fifty seconds. Joseph DeAngelo had nothing to say to his victims and nothing to say for himself.

III FACE-TO-FACE
1945–2018

Chapter 14

Although news coverage of the East Area Rapist had remained limited to the local press from the 1970s to the 1980s, the arrest of Joseph DeAngelo and reporting on the extent of his crimes had a national impact. Major newspapers, like *The New York Times*, *The Washington Post*, and the *Los Angeles Times*, dove into the case. Morning talk shows and evening news broadcasts sent reporters to hang out in front of the DeAngelo house, as if it could talk to them. Little by little, the gaps in the story were filled.

Joseph DeAngelo, like many Americans, bore his father's first name. Joseph DeAngelo Sr., born in Bath, New York, had served in the US Air Force in the 1940s. In World War II, he participated in raids over Italy, France, Austria, and Germany and came home with seven oak clusters for "meritorious achievement." A newspaper article about him written in 1943 said he had been shot and wounded during a midair battle against Japanese forces. A photo illustrates the article: Joseph DeAngelo Sr. with a wide grin, proudly wearing his Air Force cap. His son, Joe Jr., would be the spitting image of him.

Before going off to war in 1941, Joseph Sr. married Kathleen DeGroat, who was originally from New York State. Their first daughter, Rebecca DeAngelo, was born in 1942. Joseph DeAngelo Jr. was born on November 8, 1945. Then came Constance DeAngelo on August 15, 1948, and finally, John DeAngelo on October 21, 1949. The four children and their mother trailed after their father to a string of military bases in Oklahoma, Washington, DC, New Jersey, Germany, and then California—specifically Rancho Cordova, near Sacramento.

Joseph Sr. wasn't around very often. In the early 1950s, he was assigned to Korea and then transferred to Florida. Back in Rancho Cordova, son "Joe" was left to take on the role of father of the family. He cared for his brothers and sisters like they were his children, preparing their meals, taking them to school in the morning, and picking them up in the afternoon.

During this time, their mother waited tables at a Denny's restaurant. She started going out with a welder from the southern part of the state. The DeAngelos moved regularly in Rancho Cordova. All their furniture was leased. The cupboards, armoires, children's bunk beds, even the radio. Nothing belonged to them.

Joseph Jr. was a boy always looking for a new home. He often latched onto other families as if he were a part of them. For a while, he even called the parents of one of his friends "Mom" and "Dad." After high school, he shipped out to Vietnam with the Navy. He spent three years assigned to a missile-launcher warship named the USS *Canberra*, which sailed along the seventeenth parallel—the border between North and South Vietnam. When DeAngelo finished his tour, the local press announced his return to the United States. The photo accompanying the article shows him in his sailor dress whites, a rolled, black silk neckerchief tied around his collar with a square knot.

In the years that followed, he pursued his studies. In 1972, he earned an undergraduate degree in criminal justice, specializing in criminal law at Cal State, Sacramento. Right after that, he began a six-month internship at the Roseville Patrol Identification and Investigation

Divisions. Roseville was a town just north of Citrus Heights in Sacramento County.

During these years, he also met Sharon Huddle. At twenty years old, she was seven years his junior. She had a high school diploma from San Juan High School and an undergraduate degree from American River College. As was his habit, DeAngelo worked his way into her family. Only a few months after they met, Joe even moved in with Sharon's brother, James Huddle, who lived in Citrus Heights. The two often spent time together. Sometimes they flew over the region in a biplane. Other times, they went hunting or rode motocross.

DeAngelo and Sharon married in 1973. That same year, DeAngelo accompanied his mother and sister to Exeter, a small farming town in Tulare County in the southern part of the state, until his wife could join them. In Exeter, DeAngelo landed a position in the police department. It was a small, rural police force with only a few officers. They were almost a little family in uniform, in which Joseph DeAngelo distinguished himself immediately by being sarcastic, standoffish, and serious. Rarely did he laugh at his fellow officers' jokes. He seemed to want to create distance, intellectually, between himself—as an officer with a college degree—and the other officers—field cops, who just viewed this work as a job.

To mark his hiring on the force, the local paper ran the headline "Navy Veteran Serves Exeter as Policeman." The article quoted Joe's statement, which sounded a little pompous for that kind of place. "Without law and order, there can be no government, and without democratic government, there can be no freedom. Law enforcement is my career, and my job is serving the community."

In any case, being a cop on the Exeter police force was not DeAngelo's ultimate professional goal. After hours, he enrolled in courses at the Kings County Public Safety Academy. Some of the courses were taught at the College of the Sequoias in Visalia, a town just outside of Exeter, and where, since April 1974—a little less than a year after Joe's arrival—the residents' lives had been upended by the movement of a strange, roaming burglar. He ransacked houses and vandalized family portraits, amused himself with women's underwear, and stole trinkets while appearing uninterested in objects of value.

On September 11, 1975, he also killed a man while trying to kidnap his daughter. That man was Claude Snelling, a journalism professor at the College of the Sequoias in Visalia—the same college where Joe was taking courses.

The local police were soon overwhelmed by the Snelling case and approached departments in neighboring towns for assistance. Exeter was one of those towns, and the police force accepted willingly. In this way, Joseph DeAngelo found himself participating in the hunt for the Visalia Ransacker. But it was only token assistance since the burglar-killer had disappeared from the region in December 1975 after narrowly escaping capture by Detective William McGowen and after his police sketch had been disseminated to the public.

A few months later, Joseph DeAngelo also moved. He'd been hired as an officer in Auburn, a town just a short half hour from Rancho Cordova and Sacramento County. When DeAngelo showed up for duty, he had lost weight and was sporting a mustache. New town, new face.

For her part, Sharon had just been accepted at the McGeorge School of Law in center city Sacramento, where she was studying to be an attorney. The spouses slept in separate bedrooms but had a third room where they could be together. Sharon claimed that this was because she studied late at night. In addition, since being hired by the police force in Auburn, Joe worked staggered shifts.

At the Auburn police station, DeAngelo quickly earned himself the nickname "Junk Food Joey" for his penchant for potato chips and soda. He was open with other officers, but not too much; an effective officer, but not too much. Nick Willick, who was patrol sergeant at the time, would later remember DeAngelo as "an average cop who never had a significant arrest or citation."

Shortly after DeAngelo started working there, a case concerning nearby Visalia shook the county. A man had been breaking into the homes of women in the region, sexually assaulting them, and then vanishing into the night. The media nicknamed him the East Area Rapist. The residents of Rancho Cordova, Citrus Heights, and Carmichael, the three towns where most of the crimes had been committed, were living in fear.

James Huddle, Joe's brother-in-law, lived in that area. He was concerned about his wife and daughter. Two women had been raped only a few blocks from his house. The neighbors had installed floodlights on their lawns, changed the locks on the doors, and installed bars at the windows. Huddle did the same. He also purchased a pistol, which he kept under his pillow at night.

One day, he asked Joe to come check out his security setup, and the two of them went through the house together. Joe examined the bolts on the doors and verified that they worked properly, tugged on the bars at the windows to make sure they were solid, tested each security measure his brother-in-law had put in place, then turned to him and told him confidently, "You've got nothing to worry about." However, the number of crimes continued to climb. By July 1979, the East Area Rapist's victims numbered fifty. Then everything stopped, just like in Visalia.

The following August, Joseph DeAngelo was fired from his position as a police officer in Auburn. It was a strange story. On July 21, while wandering the aisles in a store, DeAngelo stuck a container of dog repellent and a Stanley hammer into his belt under his T-shirt. An employee saw him stealing and, with a coworker, asked him to accompany them to the back of the store. DeAngelo acted offended. He shouted that he would not follow them and he had stolen nothing. He tried to leave, but the two employees grabbed him by the arms. DeAngelo struggled, yelled, and even faked a heart attack, forcing the two men to release their hold. Then DeAngelo sprinted to the door before they could catch him and tie him to a chair.

Moments later, DeAngelo told the employees that he'd hit his head and suffered a concussion. He said he didn't feel well and was about to vomit. He gave his first and last name and said things that didn't make sense. Once they had confirmed his identity as an Auburn police officer, they released him. But DeAngelo's relief was short-lived.

A month after the episode, he was fired. He took it badly, filing a complaint against his supervisors, accusing them of harassment. He claimed to have suffered psychological harm since being let go. To anyone who would listen, he insisted that he had stolen nothing, sometimes adding that he was going to kill his supervisor, Lieutenant Willick. He confided this to his brother-in-law, James Huddle, and to the therapist who was overseeing the investigation of his complaint.

A while later, Nick Willick woke up at home late one night to find his granddaughter sleeping at the foot of his bed. The next morning, she was still frightened by her memory of the previous night: a man watching her as she slept. The police chief could find no trace of breaking and entering or any attempt at intrusion into the house. Then he glanced down at the ground. Right under the window, he saw two footprints in the flower bed.

Joseph DeAngelo was now thirty-three years old. Without employment, he was free to roam when and where he wanted, for example, beyond Sacramento to the southern part of the state—near Long Beach, where his wife Sharon sometimes had to go in her capacity as a lawyer. Long Beach is a coastal town near Los Angeles, a short drive from Dana Point and Irvine, where the Harrington and Manuela Witthuhn couples would soon be murdered.

In September 1981, DeAngelo's wife Sharon gave birth to a little girl, then five years later, on November 26, 1986, a second one. A third daughter was born on May 14, 1989. According to everyone, Joseph DeAngelo was a loving father who took his daughters boating, drove them to their music lessons and riding lessons, and took an interest in their schoolwork.

For a while, DeAngelo worked for the Pacific Gas and Electric Company as a diver, then took a training course paid for by the state to become a truck mechanic. He found a job at Save Mart's Distribution Center in Roseville, a town next to Sacramento. He showed up every day, was never sick, and was always meticulous. The family now lived in Citrus Heights in a beige house with red brick columns.

This family life ended in 1991 when the couple separated. But even after that, DeAngelo remained close to his in-laws, calling them "Mom" and "Dad." He also continued hanging out with his brother-in-law, James. The two men spent hours together assembling their remote-controlled model boats.

But James had never felt completely at ease with Joe, who seemed perpetually restrained. James couldn't help noticing that DeAngelo never showed affection. Never kissed, never praised. Joe always seemed to erect physical barriers between himself and others. He even had an expression that he'd pull out when he saw people kissing in public—"No PDA here," meaning public displays of affection.

The neighbors shared this image of DeAngelo, seeing him as a man difficult to figure out. The DeAngelo house was impeccably maintained, inside and out. The dishes were always done, the bathroom scrubbed, and the front lawn with its three small boulders was manicured. With military rigor, people said. The neighbors often saw him bent over, working on the lawn. Some called him "Crazy Joe." Others called him the "Freak." Still others, the "Grouch" because he yelled when he argued with his ex-wife, yelled when a neighborhood dog started barking too loudly, and sometimes yelled for no apparent reason.

Grant Gorman, the son of his next-door neighbor, was a witness on this subject. He sometimes saw DeAngelo pacing back and forth outside at night by himself. Gorman could hear him muttering obscenities and mortal threats like "I'm gonna kill them." For a long time, Grant and his family told themselves that was just

Joe, a grumpy old man who lived next door and was a little crazy.

Until the day they received a message on their telephone answering machine with no greeting or identification, though they recognized the voice. "If you don't shut that dog up, I'll deliver a load of death." A few weeks later, their Rottweiler died of a strange muscular weakness that had come over him suddenly.

Chapter 15

Could Joseph DeAngelo have been stopped during his period of criminality? Could law enforcement have prevented him from committing all these acts? Were there moments when it would have been possible to crack the facade of respectability to detect the serial rapist and killer behind it?

Since his identity was unveiled, the people who pursued or were in frequent contact with the murderer have had to live with these questions. James Huddle, as he reexamined his life as DeAngelo's ex-brother-in-law, for example. Sharon's brother did identify a few moments that had always left him feeling uneasy.

One of them was the day in the early 1970s when he and DeAngelo were driving down Auburn Boulevard to

Sacramento. DeAngelo cut off another car, whose driver responded by riding his tail. DeAngelo stuck his arm out the window and gave them the finger, then veered off into a McDonald's parking lot. The other car followed. Two men got out. As they approached him, DeAngelo pulled out a .357 revolver and threatened the men, who turned tail without a word. On the way home, the silence weighed between the two brothers-in-law. Huddle had the feeling that DeAngelo really would have shot the two men.

Another memory came back to him. DeAngelo watched television, even horror movies, with his daughters. The only thing he forbade them to watch was documentaries about serial killers or unsolved crimes.

But to understand what kind of man Joseph DeAngelo really was, we might have to go back further. In spring 1969, the future Golden State Killer had not yet committed any crimes, wasn't yet a police officer, and wasn't yet going out with Sharon Huddle. He was twenty-three years old, a young man just back from Vietnam, when he met Bonnie Colwell, who was eighteen years old.

She was from a family of academics and brilliant children. Her father was a principal at a difficult high school in Sacramento, and her brothers had all been class presidents. Bonnie had been valedictorian of her high school class and was now in her second year of studying science at Sierra College, a community college north of Sacramento, in Rocklin. She was a member of Alpha Gamma Sigma—an honor society whose motto was "Add Good Character, Knowledge, and Judgment." In her free time, she thought nothing of driving an hour to the Navy Hospital in Oakland to visit with soldiers who had come back broken from the absurd war in Southeast Asia.

When DeAngelo saw her for the first time, she was busy taking care of the science department menagerie at Sierra College. A great horned owl with noble bearing was perched on her shoulder, and a starling flitted about. Young Joe DeAngelo, with broad shoulders and light brown hair combed to one side, told her that he would like to know more about these birds and a little more about her. The young woman was intrigued and answered his questions with a smile.

In the days that followed, Joseph stopped by the lab frequently. He sat with Bonnie, and Bonnie told him about her life, including the animals she cared for at the college, her family of intellectuals, and their house in the country only about ten minutes away. At the end of the week, he asked her out, and she accepted.

DeAngelo sometimes talked about Vietnam. He showed her his left index finger, cut off halfway down, as soon as he could, telling her that it had been shot off by an enemy bullet in the Mekong Delta. But the truth was that he'd lost it by sawing it off by accident while on duty as a repairman on a warship that had been damaged in combat.

The couple enjoyed going on walks at Folsom Lake, a few miles from Sacramento. That's where DeAngelo taught Bonnie how to snorkel. He also gave her a .22-gauge long rifle, a model both precise and dangerous, and took Bonnie hunting. Sometimes he let her drive his electric blue Plymouth Road Runner, an exceedingly long car with an engine that made monstrous noise. He also owned a Honda motorcycle, which he loved to push to top speed.

To his delight, Bonnie sometimes grew scared while they were riding. When her arms tightened around his waist, he accelerated more. He loved to show that he was beyond the rules that governed ordinary mortals. And above the law. He jumped private fences and shot vultures. One day, when they were being chased by a German shepherd, Joe gave the dog a ferocious kick in the neck. The animal dropped dead in its tracks. In the intimacy of the bedroom, sex was exhausting and often painful for Bonnie. Joe was insatiable and insensitive to what Bonnie might say or how she might feel.

The day Bonnie introduced Joe to her family, she was worried about how her father would react. She doubted that Stan Colwell, with his neatly combed thinning white hair and striped neckties, would appreciate her boyfriend's manners. However, the two men hit it off. Colwell was a World War II veteran and felt respect for this boy who had just come back from Vietnam.

As always with people who appealed to him, DeAngelo was soon spending as much time as possible with this adopted family. He rode their horses and picked their oranges. He took Bonnie's brothers on jaunts around the county and invited them to movies at the drive-in. One photo shows the future killer dressed in a yellow T-shirt and black jeans and standing surrounded by the whole Colwell family. Bonnie's brothers are sitting on the ground in front of DeAngelo. In the second row, Bonnie's aunt and grandmother and each has an arm around DeAngelo's shoulders.

Then came the day of their engagement. In the Roseville *Press Tribune*, dated May 14, 1970, a large photo shows Bonnie smiling. The caption reads "Church bells are going to ring," then in smaller print, "Mr. and Mrs. Stanley B. Colwell [. . .] announce the engagement of their daughter, Bonnie Jean, to Joseph James DeAngelo Jr., son of Mrs. Jack Bosanko of Auburn and Joseph DeAngelo Sr. of Korea."

Bonnie, who had dreamed of becoming a doctor, was going to pursue studies in nursing. Joe, who wanted to be a police officer, was enrolling at Cal State, Sacramento. The only problem was that the young man was not a very strong student. He wasn't making the necessary grades, so he asked Bonnie to help him cheat on his psychology exam. This was in spring 1971. She refused. She was the daughter of a teacher and had a strong sense of the value of hard work. If Joe was going to pass this exam, he would have to do it by studying.

Joe's attempt to cheat on an exam rocked the couple's relationship. In the Colwell living room, Bonnie announced to her fiancé that their relationship was over, and she returned his engagement ring. Joe left the house in a rage. On his way out to the car, he hurled the ring into the grass. Then he gunned the engine and backed out of the driveway like a shot. For days, Bonnie and her brothers searched for the ring behind the house but never found it.

Two weeks passed without any communication between the lovers. Then, as was often the case with Joseph DeAngelo, the story concluded with a nocturnal epilogue.

One night, around 2:30 A.M., Bonnie was awakened by a sound at her window. She kneeled on her bed and lifted the curtain. Joe was standing there, pointing a revolver at her. "Get dressed," he whispered. "We're going to Reno to get married." Bonnie scrambled off the bed and ran to her father's bedroom. She tore him from his sleep, yelling that Joe was outside, had a gun, and wanted to force her to marry him. They had to call the police.

Stan Colwell got up and told his daughter to hide in the bathroom. "Don't come out until I come back for you," he ordered. Then he went out to confront Joe. The two men talked for two hours before Stan came back to the bathroom where Bonnie was waiting and told her, "You can go back to bed. Joe's left." Stan Colwell never revealed what he said to Joe that evening. Bonnie would have liked to know. These last few years, Bonnie has sometimes wondered what the decades since that night might have been if, instead of wanting to handle the situation himself, her father had called the police.

Chapter 16

Kris Pedretti's house is located at the end of a dead-end street in Elk Grove, Sacramento County. Visitors are greeted with this message on her front door: "No need to ring . . . I know you're here." So you just stand there and wait for her to open the door, then she invites you to follow her through the living room and kitchen, then out to the backyard. The trickling water of a fountain completes the serenity created by the oak trees, sycamores, and attractively landscaped shrubbery.

At the back, in the shifting light coming through the trees stands a replica of Kris's mother's tombstone. A plaque reads, "Promise that you will always remember that you are braver than you believe, stronger than you seem, and smarter than you think." A little cabin completes the ensemble, its walls inside displaying dozens of handwritten messages. "Be strong, my sister survivors." This is where Kris and other Golden State Killer victims have been meeting regularly since 2018.

The first meeting took place in Carol Daly's yard in Sacramento. Then Kris took over. At the first meeting, she introduced herself by her number. "Hello, I am victim number 10." Others had answered, "I'm number 31," "I'm number 5," "I'm the first." Today, they call one another by their first names, and each knows the story of the others.

For example, Kris told them how her father, a Marine, had decided to send her to a religious camp on the coast two days after her rape. There, she'd spent her days praying and singing "Kumbaya." When she came home, her family acted as if nothing had happened. Another woman told how, every night for years after her sister's murder, she shoved a cupboard against her bedroom window to prevent the killer from coming into her house. Still another described how her husband had gradually gone off the rails after Joe DeAngelo attacked the couple, until one night, he shot his gun at a car full of noisy teenagers driving past their house. Practically every night, terrified by the coming darkness, the couple slept over at their neighbor's house.

Kris Pedretti still sometimes meets women she doesn't know who introduce themselves as victims of Joseph DeAngelo. She sometimes wonders if the numbers tallied by the criminal justice system are correct or if there are other victims who have not been included in the total and whose stories have not been heard. And still other victims whose stories we'll never hear because they have already died.

Even when the identity of the Golden State Killer was finally uncovered, his refusal to explain himself and his motives left a lot of questions unanswered. Like Kris Pedretti, several investigators were quite sure that there were still other victims beyond those named in the indictment.

Another unknown was how DeAngelo had chosen his targets. Based on what criteria? Among them were teenagers; adults; women with blonde, chestnut, and dark hair; women who were single, cohabitating, married; and women who were in the upper middle class and working class.

The question of accomplices is also unresolved. One victim, while blindfolded, confirmed hearing DeAngelo say, "Here, put that in the car." Another one thought she'd heard two distinct voices in the house and a vehicle honk several times out front, as if summoning the attacker. A third woman, in her statement to the police, quoted her attacker as saying, "My buddy is waiting for me in the car." Was he just trying to confuse them to cover his tracks, or did he really have an accomplice with him on some of his incursions? A former detective who had worked on the case confirms that he recognized one of DeAngelo's relatives in a sketch of the Golden State Killer drawn by a victim. But the suspect died in 2019 without ever having been interrogated.

Another unanswered question: Why did Joseph DeAngelo stop killing in 1981, restart in 1986, and then stop again that same year, apparently for good? Those two years correspond to the years when his first two daughters were born. Many think their arrival either had a psychological impact on him or meant he was too busy with newborns to have time for committing crimes.

Ken Clark, who arrested DeAngelo, leans toward Michelle McNamara's hypothesis. He explains that 1986 marked the beginning of DNA in investigations. A criminal who had served on the police force must have understood what that meant. From then on, escaping justice would be much more difficult.

After April 27, 2018, several public hearings took place in Sacramento. The judge and district attorney debated some of the procedures requested by the DA, including collecting DeAngelo's DNA and photographing him naked to assess the size of his penis, which victims had so often described as abnormally small.

On August 13, 2018, DeAngelo was indicted for a thirteenth murder, that of Claude Snelling, the journalism professor in Visalia. Unable to indict DeAngelo for rapes committed decades earlier due to the statute of limitations, the Sacramento and Contra Costa County prosecutors brought charges of attempted kidnapping for the crimes where DeAngelo had moved his bound victims to other rooms in the house. These offenses carried no statute of limitations and were punishable by life imprisonment. On August 21, 2018, Joseph DeAngelo was indicted on thirteen counts of attempted kidnapping.

The defendant attended some of the public hearings, sometimes standing in a cage with bars, always dressed in an orange jumpsuit. His face had thinned considerably since his arrest. The man who had been described as having round cheeks and a thick neck now had hollow temples and loose skin at his throat. His mouth was always half-open, and on the rare occasions when he spoke, his voice was so weak that the court personnel could barely hear him.

Anne Marie Schubert, the Sacramento County district attorney, distrusted this new Joseph DeAngelo.

She was convinced that the defendant was just creating a new role for himself. If he had previously succeeded in presenting himself as a haughty police officer, loving father, and secretive neighbor, why not a senile old man?

On June 1 and June 17, 2020, Joseph DeAngelo showed up to his hearings in a wheelchair, but Schubert's hunch was borne out by security videos of his cell that same day. They showed a man altogether different. In the first video, he was standing up and doing stretching exercises, as if getting ready to start a workout. The second video showed him climbing up on his bed and stepping onto his desk to put a piece of cardboard over the lights to dim his cell.

On June 29, 2020, the issue at hand was concluding the plea bargain between the defendant and the prosecutors and the judge. To avoid having four of the five county prosecutors call for the death penalty, DeAngelo would have to plead guilty to thirteen counts of murder and thirteen counts of attempted kidnapping. In addition, he would have to admit to fifty rapes. He would also have to confess to being the East Area Rapist, the Visalia Ransacker, the Original Night Stalker, and the Golden State Killer. For the judge, this agreement would have the advantage of avoiding a long, costly, and complex trial during the COVID-19 pandemic. Joseph DeAngelo would be saving his own life.

During the entire summer day of the arraignment, the serial killer, looking haggard, listened to the judge and prosecutors walk through his list of "accomplishments" as a serial killer and rapist. In a low voice, he mumbled "Guilty" to the murders and attempted kidnappings, then "I admit" for the rapes. While the murder victims were referred to by name, the rape victims were referred to as "Jane Doe" to protect their privacy. Kris Pedretti and some of the other victims decided to rise and remain standing as their story was read.

Two months later, on August 18, 2020, the victims had the opportunity to address their attacker directly in the courtroom, if they wished. Each victim stood before the Sacramento County Superior Court at the witness stand and began telling their story, their eyes locked on the old man in the orange jumpsuit. One of them brought along a sign that summarized their collective state of mind: "Now we . . . have the power and control."

When it was her turn, Kris Pedretti, dressed in black, introduced herself. She recounted the whole evening of December 18, 1976. "I was a normal fifteen-year-old girl. I liked going to school, sleepovers at friends' houses, and going to church. It was a week before Christmas. [. . .] My world was small, predictable, and safe. That night, my world changed. [. . .] The following morning, I woke up knowing that I would never be a child again. And even if I was happy to be alive still, I felt like I was dead inside."

She added, "I find it incredibly ironic that Joe DeAngelo has daughters and a granddaughter. No sons. No grandsons. If I could talk to Joe DeAngelo, I would say to him, 'Imagine your wife, your daughters, your granddaughter at fifteen years of age, imagine them tied up and blindfolded while they are being raped, tortured, and feeling mortally threatened by some unknown masked man who has the right of life or death over them while he rapes them for hours [. . .] Do you have any remorse for doing that to me? [. . .] There is no prayer strong enough to save you.'"

DeAngelo remained impassive as he sat facing her. He would also remain impassive the next day when another woman declared "May he rot in hell" before stating that she had brought a friend along. Her name was Bonnie Colwell. Not being a crime victim, she could not speak. But this woman spoke for her. "If Bonnie were allowed to address you," she said, "she would tell you that [. . .] not even a gun could make her marry you. When she saw who you really were, she was done with you [. . .] When you begin to pay your time, you will go back to a lost and insignificant place and disappear from her life forever. Amen."

The day the verdict was delivered was August 21. Joseph DeAngelo appeared in court one last time. The prosecutors from eight California counties and the lawyers were all there. Kris Pedretti and the "Jane Does" and their relatives, as well as a dozen other victims, were also there. Carol Daly and Paul Holes were there.

DeAngelo's relatives, who had almost never spoken since his arrest, wrote letters that would be read by the defendant's lawyers. DeAngelo's sister Rebecca, wrote that her "love for Joe will never end" and blamed a difficult childhood with a "hard" father who was "physically and mentally abusive" toward her brother and mother. "Joe faced so many things. [. . .] Of course, it will never justify what happened."

His eldest daughter said he "is the best father that [she] could have had." "I could never tell you all that my father has meant to me. [. . .] He took care of the people he loved, his friends and his family, and has always been generous and considerate. [. . .] My father had so much love, kindness, and empathy for others. [. . .] He taught me to appreciate life, never to take things for granted. I can't tell you how much my daughter and I have been grieving since he's no longer in our lives."

Finally, for the first time since the beginning of the hearings, Joseph DeAngelo rose and spoke. At first, hunched over, then he slowly straightened up. He remained standing for a moment before taking off his COVID mask in a gesture that was slow and dramatic. His voice low, he said, articulating clearly, "I have listened to all your testimonies. Each one of 'em. And I am truly sorry. Thank you, Your Honor." And sat down. That was it.

For his victims, it was a slap in the face. Forty-four years of waiting for "I am truly sorry," uttered without conviction, like an obligation.

Now it was Judge Michael Bowman's turn to speak. He condemned Joseph DeAngelo to eleven life sentences with no possibility of parole, to be served consecutively, plus fifteen life sentences with the possibility of parole, plus eight additional years of incarceration. The rapist and serial killer was not condemned to death, but he might as well have been. He would serve out his sentences in the Corcoran State Prison in California, reputedly one of the hardest in the country—where he would no doubt die.

When DeAngelo was led out of the courtroom, the victims all stood up, and suddenly, the courtroom rang with their applause. They clapped so hard that observers and the media left the killer to his sad fate and turned to concentrate on the women.

Placer County, Spring 2022

To find Richard Shelby, you have to drive forty minutes north from Sacramento, deep into Placer County. Far from the freeways and other major arteries, this is gold rush country, crisscrossed by narrow, unpaved roads. After you drive up a small slope, a dirt road leads you to his ranch. The nearest neighbors are hundreds of yards away.

The former cop came up here to live with his wife and two children after leaving Rancho Cordova in the late 1970s. Since retiring, he spends his days among the geese, ducks, and cats, working his farm, including the mandarin oranges he sells and the rosemary he dries in his attic. He reads a lot too. Recently, he dove into *The Odyssey* as a chance to confirm that the world hasn't really changed in the past thousands of years.

In April 2018, it was Carol Daly who broke the news to him and others that the Golden State Killer had finally been identified. Shelby received the call at five o'clock in the morning. As always, his response was restrained. On the one hand, he felt immense satisfaction, knowing the man he had pursued for years, and the criminal who had visited him one night and frightened his son, had finally been arrested. On the other hand, he couldn't help feeling a rush of disappointment, even shame, for not having been the one to figure it out.

The name Joseph DeAngelo had never appeared on any of the lists of suspects. Briefly, Shelby had considered going to the hearings to look DeAngelo "straight in the eye." Something in him would have liked to plumb that gaze and verify that the face was completely unknown to him. In the end, he decided against it. The killer would never have said what he wanted to hear, anyway. So, Shelby followed the proceedings from afar, through the news. On August 21, 2020, after learning that DeAngelo had been condemned to multiple life sentences, Shelby went back to his mandarin oranges, rosemary, and geese. He turned the page on this case, once and for all.

Really, he'd done that two years earlier. The day after the Golden State Killer was arrested in 2018, Shelby had spent hours going through his house from top to bottom. He'd checked every drawer and every closet and collected every file relating to the case, copies of police reports, photos, loose pages filled with notes, memos, USB keys, and CDs; all the leads to his cursed investigation. Piling it all into his tractor, he climbed up behind the wheel and drove out to a little hill on the other side of the orchard. There, he gathered all the material into a pile about three feet high. Then he scraped a match, leaned over the pile to light it, and watched the fire take. The way he remembers it, the police reports were the first to catch fire. Soon, the rest of it had all gone up in smoke.

APPENDICES

CHRONOLOGY OF CRIMES

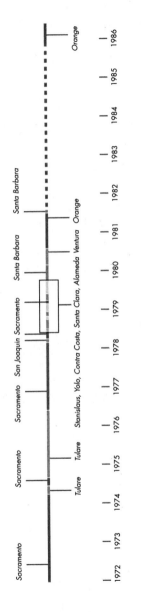

MAP OF CALIFORNIA

MAP OF THE GOLDEN STATE KILLER'S FIRST TEN VICTIMS

Sources

Huddle, James. *Killers Keep Secrets: The Golden State Killer's Other Life*. Published by the author, 2020.

McNamara, Michelle. *Et je disparaîtrai dans la nuit*. Translated by Estelle Roudet. Kero, 2018, and *Le Livre de Poche*, 2019. Originally published as *I'll Be Gone in the Dark* (Harper Collins, 2018).

Shelby, Richard. *Hunting a Psychopath: The East Area Rapist/Original Night Stalker Investigation*. Published by the author, 2014.

St. John, Paige, "Man in the Window" articles, *Los Angeles Times*, 2019.

The other sources are long interviews with the protagonists of this book and police reports dating from the relevant years.

Acknowledgments

For my immersion in the story of the winding, carefree streets of Sacramento County that were so brutally bloodied in the 1970s, I would like to thank, first and foremost, Richard Shelby, former police lieutenant. He spent long hours with me at his remote California home and sacrificed his peaceful retirement to return to the hellish investigation to establish the Golden State Killer's identity. His remarkable memory, his generosity, and his care in responding to each of my questions supported me throughout my own investigation.

Sincere thanks also go to his colleague, former Deputy Sheriff Carol Daly. Despite the violence of this investigation and the scars she still carries, she was willing to tell me about life behind the scenes in the sheriff's department during the frantic hunt for the monsters that occupied her daily life. She lent wonderful support to the victims for over forty years and set such an example for so many women that she deserves a book focusing on her story.

Many thanks also to Sergeant Ken Clark. He was my eyes for the final hours of Joseph DeAngelo's freedom. I hope he is now taking advantage of his retirement far from the beating sun in California and savoring the permanent rains in Washington State.

These women agreed to relive the long hours of their terrible night and the tainted decades that followed. I can't imagine how difficult it was for them to dig back into those nightmarish memories; I know it was a sacrifice for them. My deepest thanks to Kris Pedretti and Gay Hardwick. I hope the victim numbers attached to them for over forty years will fade somewhat with DeAngelo's incarceration.

I would also like to thank Sacramento County District Attorney Anne Marie Schubert for finding several hours to spend with me in her already packed schedule.

My thanks also to Michelle Cruz and Jennifer Carol, the sister and daughter of victims of the Original Night Stalker, for their help and patience.

I would like to offer journalist Paige St. John my congratulations for the work and the research she did on this case for the *Los Angeles Times*. Her efforts helped me considerably in my own work.

A bouquet of thanks to my mother and my sister, whose vacation I ruined with this story of a serial murderer.

Finally, sincere thanks to three people without whom this book would not exist: my editor, Elsa Delachair, and Franck Annese and Stéphane Régy of So Press. Elsa, I treasure your advice and your confidence in me and appreciate your tolerance for my delayed email responses. Franck and Stéphane, thank you for everything. I would never be the journalist I am today without having had the opportunity to work with you.

About the Author

William Thorp is a reporter for *Vakita*, a French digital news media publication focusing on social issues and the environment. Previously, he was a journalist at *Society*, a news magazine, where, for five years, he covered stories in North America, Europe, and Africa. He started out investigating human interest stories in France before writing articles and long-form content while on international assignment.

CRIME INK PRESENTS

FRANCE'S LEADING TRUE CRIME JOURNALISTS INVESTIGATE AMERICA'S MOST NOTORIOUS CASES — ONE FOR EVERY STATE IN THE UNION.

Each title revisits an infamous crime, replete with all the hard facts and gruesome details, and brings fresh new perspectives to these storied cases. Taken together, the series reveals a dark national legacy, state-by-state, from sea to shining sea . . .

NEW YORK:
THE ALICE CRIMMINS CASE
ANAÏS RENEVIER
TRANSLATED BY LAURIE BENNETT
ISBN: 978-1-61316-629-1

The case that rocked New York City in the summer of '65. Two children disappear and turn up dead. Their beautiful and promiscuous mother is convicted in the court of public opinion . . . but did she commit the crime?

CALIFORNIA:
THE GOLDEN STATE KILLER CASE
WILLIAM THORP
TRANSLATED BY LYNN E. PALERMO
ISBN: 978-1-61316-631-4

For years a methodical killer stalked the shadows of sunny California. Responsible for at least fifty assaults and thirteen murders, an unlikely modern development led to an arrest more than forty years after his reign of terror began.

OHIO:
THE CLEVELAND JOHN DOE CASE
THIBAULT RAISSE
TRANSLATED BY LAURIE BENNETT
ISBN: 978-1-61316-633-8

A body is discovered by police in 2002 . . . but it doesn't match its name. The deceased had assumed a false identity. Who was he really? And what other secrets was he hiding?